Betty White's Pet-Love

Betty White's Pet-Love

How Pets Take Care of Us

BY BETTY WHITE

WITH

THOMAS J. WATSON

William Morrow and Company • New York • 1983

Library of Congress Catalog Card Number: 83-61737

ISBN: 0-688-02207-3

Printed in the United States of America

First Edition

1 2 3 4 5 6 7 8 9 10

BOOK DESIGN BY LINEY LI

For Allen Ludden . . .

MY HEART

• Acknowledgments •

It was Tess and Horace White and their love of animals that made this project possible. They taught me from day one that the enrichment and compassion we receive from animals can be spread outward to everyone we contact, without our even being conscious of it.

And if Mom and Dad sowed the seed for the book, it was my collaborator, Tom Watson, and our agents, Sherry Robb and Bart Andrews, who helped bring it to fruition.

Some books, I've been told, seem to write themselves. This, alas, wasn't one of them . . . we had plenty of help. We would, therefore, at this point like to give credit where it is so richly deserved.

Generous assistance was offered by each of the following individuals: Dart Anthony, International Humane Society; Phil Arkow, Humane Society of the Pikes Peak Region; John Behrens, CBS-TV; Dr. Leo Bustad, Dean of the College of Veterinary Medicine, Washington State University; Suzanne Crouch, Latham Foundation; Patricia Curtis, author; Ralph Dennard, Hearing Dog Program, San Francisco SPCA; Liz Helms, Ahead with Horses, Inc.; Linda M. Hines, People-Pet Partnership Program, Washington State University; Frances Joswick, Orange County Riding Center; Maria W. Kyne, Riding for the Handicapped of Western Pennsylvania; David Lee, Lima State

Hospital for the Criminally Insane; Juana P. Lyon, Companion Animal Association of Arizona; Lida L. McCowan, Cheff Center for the Handicapped; Michael McCulloch, psychiatrist; William McCulloch, Texas A & M University; Christine McParland, North American Riding for the Handicapped Association; Peter R. Messent, Society for Companion Animal Studies, Great Britain; Pat Prescott, Delaware Humane Association; Kathy Quinn, Purdy Prison Partnership Program; Alamo Reaves, Handi-Dogs, Inc.; Samuel B. Ross, Jr., Green Chimneys Farm; Tracy Hartley Smith, Canine Companions for Independence; Betsy Solfisburg, Pets Are Wonderful Council; Flossie Stowell, photographer; Marlene Walsh, American Humane Association; Leonard Warner, North American Riding for the Handicapped Association; Ken White, San Francisco SPCA; Kris Winship, American Humane Association; and Patti Zangle, Green Chimneys Farm.

A personal note of thanks to my friends Tom Sullivan, Doris Day, Roddy MacDowall, Loretta Swit, Earl Holliman, Gretchen Wyler, Jimmy and Gloria Stewart, Bob Barker, Edith Head, Jock and Betty Leslie-Melville, and Mary Tyler Moore, for *always* sharing with me their love and zest for animals.

Grateful appreciation is also extended to friends Wallace Jamie and Hugh Thebault of the Latham Foundation for their ongoing assistance in various endeavors.

Special thanks are extended to Richard Brock, for reading and commenting on the manuscript as we went along . . . and for his constant support throughout.

And last, an official salute to Dr. Boris Levinson, whose research and work during the past thirty years has laid the foundation for the human/companion animal bond. Where would we be without him?

• Contents •

Appendices:

• Prologue •

I have been having fun for years . . . working and playing and living with animals. Not a day goes by that my life is not enriched by my two dogs, Timothy and Sooner, or by T.K. ("Timmy's Kitty"), a black cat who has moved in unannounced but is here to stay. These three make the good times better and the bad times more bearable.

Timothy, I should explain, is a coal-black miniature poodle, and Sooner, our foundling, we like to think of as a Labrador/golden retriever mix. There may have been another casual friend or two in there somewhere as well, but who's counting. My husband, Allen Ludden, and I found Sooner one night on Sunset Boulevard where, witnesses said, he had been thrown out of a van. Many people know my weakness, but oddly enough it was Allen who insisted we take him home. Hence, the name Sooner—we'd sooner take him home than leave him where he was. Corny, but oh, so true. And I've been grateful for him every second of the twelve years he's been with me.

Sooner and Tim are known to their intimates as "the odd couple," but the name is just as appropriate for Timmy and T.K. These two darlings—dog and cat—play together like twins. T.K. even rolls on her back and lets Tim try to scratch her tummy. What a pair! Of course, T.K.'s relationship with Sooner is much more typical. . . .

"When did you first become so fascinated by animals?" That question is almost invariably in the top three, along with "How did you get started in show business?" and "What is Mary Tyler Moore really like?"

My stock answer regarding the start of my interest in animals—"in the womb"—may sound glib and superficial, but it is the absolute truth. Animals have always been a way of life with my family. I never thought of myself as an "only child," because our pets were my playmates and confidants. I cannot remember any family high spot, or crisis, or joy, or sorrow that didn't include whatever pets we had at the time. More than once in my life I have dried my tears on soft silky ears!

Explaining *when* I first became interested in animals is a pleasure. What puzzles me, however, is having to explain *why*. "Why do you expend so much time and energy and resources on animals? Why not on people?"

To me the answer is so very simple: Helping the one does not preclude helping the other. Behaviorists tell us, and this is fact not theory, that the way a person treats and interacts with animals has a great bearing on how he treats other people.

I suppose, in the final analysis, I have invested a lot of time and love in animals over the years. But I have reaped such a great return on each investment. This was never more true than eighteen months ago when my Allen died.

Life does not come equipped with an instruction manual, and neither does death. Allen and I had worked together on and off during almost eighteen years of marriage (lacking three days), but in our private life we were *always* very much a team. As well as lovers, we were each other's critic, editor, fan, and friend. While we had had two long years to get used to the idea, when he died I was shattered. My first instinct was to crawl away somewhere to mourn in private, and to some extent I suppose I did. But there were these two other gentlemen in my life, Timmy and Sooner (T.K. hadn't moved in yet); they missed Allen, too, and were not about to let me just wither away.

Pets, I discovered long ago, always seem to know what a person is feeling. After Allen's death there was a wonderful outpouring of love and sympathy from our family and friends, all the people we had worked with over the years, plus hundreds of people we had never met, but who had come to know how special he was through watching him on television. My mother was incredible in her support, knowing just when to move in, and when to stand back and give me the little space I needed. But still, whenever anybody was around, even those who were the closest, I felt obligated—to keep up appearances and try not to show my grief. I suppose that was from not wanting to make them feel even sadder worrying about me. Such games we humans play! Of course I was grieving! My life had been torn apart! And while I was able to put on a great show of strength for my friends and family, I could not pull the same act with Timothy and Sooner. They knew me too well; they could read me loud and clear.

Sensing that Allen's death had left me badly wounded, Timothy and Sooner snuggled in to help. Not that I was so willing to cooperate, at least at first. But can anyone say no to a little black pest who keeps throwing his favorite toy at you, or to a seventy-pound leaner who is adamant that dinner is already thirty minutes late?

I had continued to work right up until three days before Allen's death, beginning and ending each day at the hospital. All at once the pattern changed, and the purpose was gone. I had no interest in "lights, camera, makeup," or much of anything else for that matter. It was, therefore, up to Sooner and Timothy to take over organizing my day. Their needs became my needs. They gave my life definition—a reason to get up in the morning, a firm grasp on today when so much of me wanted to turn back the clock to yesterday.

Timothy and Sooner got me through that first week, the first month, the first year—all those terrible "firsts." And now it has been eighteen months since Allen's death. I have discovered that while I can never forget such a loss, I have, with time, pulled my life together. I am working full tilt, exploring new activities, taking new challenges.

Allen, of course, is still such an important part of my life, a constant topic of conversation, and indeed, an integral part of this book. It was he who for years had encouraged me to get something down in print about the love, the companionship, and yes, the therapy, that pets provide. Now, I'm ready. . . .

• Part One •

You, Me, and the Animals We Live With

"Understanding is the Keys to the Kingdom. . . ."
—DR. MICHAEL FOX

1.

Introducing . . .
The Human/Animal Bond

This is a book about love. It's about you and me and the animals we live with. Unlike other books you may have read, it does not deal with how people should take care of animals but rather with how pets *do* take care of us.

That's right, *take care of us*! Recent findings have made it reasonable to believe that owning a pet may improve our physical and mental health. As television news reporter Harry Reasoner put it, "It seems that man's best friend in some cases may turn out to be man's best medicine."

Well! I've always known I love having animals . . . What a surprise to find something you love is neither immoral nor fattening but *good* for you!

But good they are. Pets have been found to lower a person's blood pressure, reduce stress, provide an outlet for playing, cause people to exercise, and promote feelings of intimacy, continuity, security, and general well-being. Experiments have found animals to be helpful in accelerating the learning process in children, providing senior citizens with self-assurance and reasons for living, and aiding many people outside the mainstream of society—prisoners, the retarded, the mentally and physically ill, the handicapped, and the hospitalized.

If we were to take a poll, we would probably find that

everyone who has ever owned a pet, from society matron to welfare child, has had his life enriched in one way or another. It matters not that some owners lead their pets around on a rhinestone-studded leash while others use an old piece of clothesline from the backyard. What is important is that something scientists are calling "the human/animal bond" is present in all instances, and the effect that pets have on their owners is of value.

Animals have always been a part of my family, yet, until recently, I had never heard the phrase "human/animal bond." It seems to be the new "in" term for a relationship that has been around for a long, long time.

The affiliation between man and animal has been more or less an accepted fact through the ages—sometimes more, sometimes less. The bond itself has existed since the first cave man *(must* I say cave person?) carried an orphaned jackal cub back to his home fireside and discovered they both felt better for the contact. . . .

Centuries later, members of the royal court of ancient China (emperor and concubine alike) carried their tiny dogs about with them, tucked into their sleeves for comfort. . . .

Cats were so important to ancient Egyptians that when the pet died, the entire family shaved off their eyebrows in mourning. . . .

The beloved spaniels of England's King Charles II were his constant companions, and they kept the vigil even as he lay dying. . . .

The list goes on . . . and on . . . and on. . . .

All through the ages, then, there have been those who have fully realized how much companion animals can mean to a person's sense of well-being. There have even been isolated individuals who have studied the subject and written about it. But man's relationship with animals has, at least until recently, existed without having a specific name or term of reference.

Approximately twenty years ago, however, scientific interest in animals began to surface, and with it arose the need to call it something. Because many individuals were working independently, we began to hear a spate of confusing terms—pet therapy, pet-facilitated therapy, pet-assisted therapy, animal-assisted therapy—none of which said it all.

With more and more attention being paid not only to the use of pets in aiding the health-impaired but to the therapeutic value of human/animal relationships in general, the term "human/animal bond" emerged and appears to be best suited to cover the entire subject. This, then, is the topic of our book.

The human/animal bond includes *all* humans, sick and well, and all types of animals—farm animals, wild animals, those used as physiological or psychological aids, as well as all the various and sundry creatures generally thought of as pets.

Scientific study of the human/animal bond is clearly an endeavor whose time has come. Everywhere we look, there are new studies, new findings, new programs that are going beyond the old whys and hows and how-to's on the subject of animals and beginning to help us understand *what* our relationship is with animals, *what* influence they have on our psyches. All over the country—indeed, the world— major universities are doing research on the therapeutic value of pets in our society, and the number of hospitals, nursing homes, prisons, and mental institutions employing full-time pet therapists (that is, therapists who are pets) is burgeoning by geometric progression. In other words, *what animal lovers have known all along has finally gone public*!

Isn't it ironic that now, when mankind is in the middle of a full-swing technological revolution, we are also beginning to take a look at our fellow creatures?

Maybe it's not so ironic. From the beginning, human and animal history have been inextricably woven together.

Early on, that first caveman and his jackal not withstanding, human/animal interaction was simple: first, "You kill me, I kill you"; then, "You serve me, I dominate you." People have used animals for food (both as hunter and huntee), for clothing, protection, transportation, even as a status symbol or rate of exchange: "I will give you four fine goats for your daughter's hand in marriage."

As the numbers increased on both sides, so did the complexities. Today, humans and animals are competing for space on our ever-shrinking planet, and the words "endangered species" have become part of our vocabulary. With modern urbanization and an ever-growing population, even our household pets stand a chance of making the threatened list. Some cities around the world have already passed laws against maintaining dogs within city limits, and here in the United States, landlords are, of necessity, putting up more and more "no pets" signs.

Perhaps this helps explain the relatively sudden, concerted interest in the human/animal bond. Human nature being what it is, we take things for granted until we are in danger of losing them. The studies now being conducted may cast new light on the *quality* of our companion-animal relationships, as opposed to merely the *quantity.*

Certainly the most important thing these studies will do is get our attention. When serious people with lots of letters after their names, and reputable old universities behind them, tell us that owning a pet can reduce our blood pressure, ease our stress, and possibly lengthen our lives . . . we listen!

Recently published marketing reports indicate that Americans spent $7.1 billion on pets and pet care in 1980, and estimate the total will grow to $10.6 billion by 1988. It might appear, at least at first glance, that we are paying a very stiff price for the luxury of maintaining a companion animal. But are we? Are they really a luxury? Let's take a closer look at what scientists say we are getting in return.

Lower Blood Pressure. Studies have shown that stroking and talking to a pet lowers a person's blood pressure.

It was established as far back as 1929 that a dog's blood pressure goes down and his heart rate decelerates while he is being petted. Now, more than fifty years later, we are learning that a similar phenomenon occurs within the person doing the petting. Kenneth White (no relation), education coordinator, San Francisco SPCA, indicates, "We've found that blood pressure and heart rate go down considerably while a person is petting a dog. It has a deeply calming effect, like prayer or meditation."

These findings have been noted and welcomed not only by the "animal community" but by other experts as well. The medical value of owning a pet was recognized at a recent annual meeting of the American Heart Association, where it was reported that reductions in blood pressure have been noted in subjects who are merely watching tropical fish or talking to birds.

Erika Friedmann, a biologist from the University of Pennsylvania, reported that in her study of heart-attack patients, one of the factors that turned out to be statistically significant—no matter how sick a patient was—was pet ownership. Even in tests excluding dogs (and the exercise involved in maintaining them) those patients with other pets showed a markedly higher rate of survival.

According to Dr. Aaron Katcher, associate professor of psychiatry, also of the University of Pennsylvania, cardiac patients and people with high blood pressure tend to live longer and live better when they have pets. "There's something about interacting with pets which is calming. When people talk to people, blood pressure tends to go up, because you always wonder how the other person's evaluating you. With pets, it's really quite different. You have trust in a pet. The pet listens. And that gives people the kind of comfort which is manifest in a decrease in tension, a loss of anxiety, a loss of stress."

A Loss of Stress. Stress—mental tension—has been identified as a major health hazard, one that contributes to both physical and mental illness. Pets have been found to dissipate some of that tension as they help people relax.

I do not need to read a research document to believe this—I only have to spend a few minutes with my own pets. Timothy and Sooner and T.K. enjoy having me home, never judge, and certainly never play such complex psychological games with me as withholding affection to induce me to act in certain ways. They are simply there—offering *unconditional* love, and receiving the same in return. So many nights I come home tired and frazzled by a long day's work, but after I'm greeted by their ecstatic faces, wagging tails, and warm purrs, the events of my day, good and bad, fall into their proper perspective. Even my feet don't hurt as much!

Patricia Curtis, pet expert and author of numerous books on the subject, knows what I mean: "One of the great rewards of life is coming home to be greeted by my dogs and cats. They're glad to see me whether I'm gone five minutes or five hours. After a bad day, it's soothing and calming to find someone who enjoys my company and is so uncritical and willing to please me."

Because the affection pets offer is unconditional, they allow us to be totally ourselves. They couldn't care less about our color, creed, gender, age, politics, nationality, or economic status. As Dr. Aline H. Kidd, professor of psychology at Mills College, puts it, companion animals give one the chance to associate with a being "who doesn't judge, doesn't argue back, doesn't have prejudices, biases, preconceptions and definitions which don't agree with yours—and, above all else, they don't 'tell on you.'"

Watching me relax with our pets, Allen said many times he would give a lot for that kind of "passion" or outside interest. He admitted that as much as he loved his garden and enjoyed working in it, his green thumb did not provide the same day-in, day-out calming diversion as did my animals.

A Reason to Play.   Timothy and Sooner and T.K. offer me a chance to unwind by playing. You remember playing . . . those joyous romps we all used to have as children. As author James Fixx says, "Although many of us virtually stop playing at some point in our lives, we never outgrow our need for it." Dr. O. Carl Simonton, medical director of the Cancer Counseling and Research Center, Fort Worth, says, "I believe play increases our creativity . . . our energy in ourselves."

We talk a great deal about our playing these days, but all too often our major sports and our jogging have become very serious business. What has happened to the fun—to the joy and sense of humor that once went along with play?

It has been well established that a chuckle or six reduces stress, even though *explaining* humor has baffled scientists through the ages. The more it is examined, the unfunnier it gets. Ask any comic. Wisely, there is a new breed of researcher less interested in what laughter *is* than what it *does*. Tests have shown that after a hearty laugh, blood pressure and heartbeat rates go down, and muscles are more relaxed.

Norman Cousins, in his *Anatomy of an Illness,* spoke emphatically of how laughter enabled him to overcome a debilitating health problem. The medical community as a whole is not quite ready to buy the idea completely, but more and more individuals are finding it worthy of investigation.

I can't help but feel that there must be a correlation between the effect of laughter and the influence of animals on the human psyche. They both take us out of ourselves, at least momentarily, which in itself can be beneficial. My unscientific conclusion is obvious: Get a funny pet—then you have all the bases covered!

A Chance to Exercise. Lack of exercise has been cited in one report after another as contributing to hypertension and coronary heart disease. Pets seldom allow one to lead a sedentary existence. Even if you are not inclined—as some of us are—to get down and roll around on the floor with your pets, just taking them out for their daily constitutional gets you up out of that easy chair and affords you a few minutes of exercise. My Timothy and I play "retrieve" and it's a great workout. I'm getting so I can fetch the ball back almost every time!

A Sense of Security. More and more, we are becoming a nation of single-member households. People are living alone, not only because of death or divorce, but by choice. Even so, when the sun goes down and memories of childhood's bogeyman start creeping into one's consciousness, it's nice to have *someone* around for security. Pets, particularly dogs, fulfill this need admirably. Timothy, for example, seems to hear every car that goes by the house. He announces loud and clear whenever one of them stops in the drive, and tells me whether or not it's someone he knows.

Similarly, strangers-with-animals seem to be less ominous than strangers alone. Admittedly, this could be a false sense of security, but nevertheless, it exists. My secretary, Pat, for example, recently confessed that she had been awakened in the middle of the night (actually, it was 6 A.M., but still very dark outside) by a passing stranger who lived down the block. When she peeked out to see who was on her doorstep, she felt an immediate relief to see that it was someone out walking his dog. The man no longer seemed so frightening, and she was ready to listen when he told her one of her sprinklers was leaking.

Political candidates have been clued in to this psychology for years—so much so that sidling up to a friendly puppy seems to be second only to kissing babies for securing public acceptance. Richard Nixon, a man whose political speeches fill volumes, will always be remembered for his 1952 "Checkers Speech." In that televised address, Nixon, then a candidate for the vice-presidency, answered charges that he had accepted funds and gifts from supporters in exchange for political favors. The speech got its name from a little cocker spaniel puppy named Checkers who had been a gift for the Nixon children from one of the candidate's backers. Checkers, Nixon told the nation, had already become a member of the family, and "whatever they say, we are going to keep her!"

It is not only strangers and people in the public eye whom we warm up to after seeing them with pets—sometimes it's our own next-door neighbors. Friends who live in metropolitan areas tell me the only neighbors they feel safe in introducing themselves to are the ones out walking their dogs. Indeed, oftentimes the dogs themselves become the ice breakers, allowing two cautious neighbors to strike up that initial conversation.

A Chance to Communicate. Pets do ease the way for many of us who are the least bit shy about being with strangers. Parties, for example, have never been one of my favorite things. It never takes me long to check out the territory and find what animals (four-legged) are on the premises. If I disappear for any length of time, I can probably be found in the kitchen or off in some corner getting acquainted with a dog or cat or bird or hamster or . . . Speaking of ice breakers, ever notice how if someone at the party brings up the subject of animals or pets, almost everyone in the room seems to have a story to contribute?

Strangers at a cocktail party aren't the only ones to benefit from "animal talk." Pets are often instrumental in improving communication between members of a family. With everyone in the modern household operating on a different schedule, communications can often break down. Too many times, the family sits down as a group to discuss something only when there is a problem—if then. They rarely talk over the events of the day just for the sheer pleasure of sharing and being together!

Dr. Boris Levinson, professor of psychology and pioneer in the field of human/animal relationships, believes very strongly that "a pet can make positive changes in family dynamics. . . . The pet bridges the generation gap between children and adults by providing a common object of responsibility."

I not only talk *about* my pets, I talk *to* them . . . or more precisely, *with* them. Animals and I have always been great communicators, right from the day my parents brought me home from the hospital and auditioned me in front of Toby, our big orange tabby cat. Luckily for me, he approved, or I probably would have been sent right back to the hospital. (Does that give you a clue as to how my folks felt about animals?) As it was, Toby condescended to perch on the corner of my crib by the hour and play watch-cat. I eventually learned I was supposed to include humans in my conversations, too—but that is still only my second language.

Whenever the opportunity presents itself—like now— I preach the gospel of how important it is for us to talk to our animals. Not just orders, but conversation. It pays off in two ways: It provides a wonderful sounding board, and more important, it keeps them tuned in to us. They may not understand our words, but they certainly catch the tone of our voices and somehow get the idea.

This communication is a two-way street—I am tuned in to them as well. Timmy, as I said, keeps me posted on who is in our driveway; Sooner, older and more sophisticated, has a vocabulary of barks that indicate the presence of bees, as opposed to crows, as opposed to helicopters, as opposed to human strangers. He also has a distinct bark that says, "I want to come in."

A Sense of Intimacy. In every article on the human/animal bond and its use in therapy, the physiological results of animal contact are mentioned. One of these is intimacy, an occasion not only to talk but to gently touch at the same time. This is easy for me to believe, without any knowledge of medicine, simply from noticing the change in myself the minute I get my hands on an animal. I relax, I can physically feel my tensions slipping away and a sense of well-being taking over.

Some people, of course, are more oriented to touch than others. I personally am an inveterate toucher. When talking with someone, I tend to emphasize a point by putting my hand on the other person's arm. When I greet people I like, I usually touch my cheek to theirs—the actual kiss I leave for close encounters of the personal kind. It isn't being phony or showbizzy to me. I am simply a *toucher*.

Buddy Hackett, by contrast, makes it abundantly clear that he can't abide being touched. His feeling must be not unlike that of a cat when some well-meaning soul strokes his fur in the wrong direction. It is interesting to sit next to Buddy on the Johnny Carson panel or *The Merv Griffin Show* and try to remember not to reach for his arm when we are all laughing at his jokes.

Author Ashley Montagu has studied people and animals and believes that most people have a strong need for physical contact. He writes, "Many individuals who, for one reason or another, experience difficulty in touching others often satisfy their tactile needs with pets."

Similarly, Dr. Samuel Corson, professor of psychiatry at Ohio State University, places a great importance on the ability of pets to fulfill the need for tactile stimulation. He says that touch is one of the first sensations that humans experience and often the last—and yet it seems to be one of the senses we take most for granted.

With me, it's like the chicken and the egg—I'm not sure whether I first liked animals because I could touch them, or whether animals taught me to like to touch. All I know is that when I see any animal I have an overwhelming desire to touch it . . . even lions and tigers and bears and—Mom forgive me—even snakes.

Allen caught on early in our relationship to my need to hold and fondle and cuddle our pets. He said I even *looked* different when I was holding an animal. He also found a way to use this fact to advantage in solving a professional problem for me—having pictures taken.

Let me explain that pictures, like parties, are not my best thing. With casual snapshots I can muddle through, and, of course, with a television camera I can keep moving, but portraits and studio photo sessions have always been a nightmare for me. Allen used to look at the proofs and say, "You're sniling! Your back teeth are locked! You don't really smile that way!"

It was Allen's idea to bring Nicky, our little black poodle (Timothy came later), to the portrait studio and sit him on my lap out of camera range. Nick loved it as an excuse to be held, and I relaxed *visibly*. That was the best set of pictures I've ever had taken, and no one ever realized why.

A Sense of Continuity. Constancy, Dr. Katcher believes, has been vastly underrated as a contributor to our mental and emotional health. He says, "Because there are no demands on pets to mature or progress . . . they do not force *us* to change." This is particularly important considering so much of contemporary society is living on shifting sands in family relationships, personal relationships, and just day-to-day existence. Just when we begin to console ourselves that our individual problems are unique and temporary, our television set comes to life to make sure we realize that it's a jungle out there. Constancy and genuine intimacy seem pretty remote.

What are we as a society doing to ourselves? Sociologists have been calling the last ten years the Me Decade. I, for one, have always been in favor of self-appreciation and self-fulfillment, but not at the expense of everything else. It seems to me that as people "found" themselves, they lost important contact with each other.

The family unit that was once the backbone of our society has certainly fallen onto hard times. The extended family, which once included not only Mom and Dad and the kids but also Grandma and Grandpa, not to mention a maiden aunt or two—all living under one roof (or at least nearby)—seems long forgotten. Each family member has increased his independence—which can be beneficial—but at a price.

In addition, families today are far more mobile than they once were. Few people seem to cultivate community ties or develop an ongoing sense of involvement (and thus, belonging) in any given neighborhood.

Dr. Levinson states that despite all this, we have a great need "for roots, for belonging, for the feeling of fulfillment and continuity." This, he maintains, "can be supplied by the pet."

Looking at my own life I see many segments: childhood, an early marriage, ten years of being a single career girl, then my life with Allen. Move in a little closer and there are segments within segments: Allen well, Allen ill

. . . our lives together with his children in New York, then just the two of us in California . . . and now I'm heading into a brand new segment, life without Allen. The point of all this introspection is that throughout the many stages of my life, my feeling for animals has been an unwavering constant . . . a dependable reservoir of comfort.

Continuity, fulfillment, companionship, lower blood pressure—possibly longer lives—these are just a few of the gifts that animals bring to us. There are certainly many more, which we will be exploring in the chapters ahead. As you read, you may note that different people are approaching various animal subjects from different perspectives. Indeed, the viewpoints and opinions of the scientific community are in a constant state of change. It was just a relatively short time ago, for example, that the authoritative consensus was against the slightest tendency to anthropomorphize—that is, to attribute human feelings and reactions to animals. Thinking of a pet as a substitute child, or even comparing humans and animals in the same breath, was considered to be a positive sign of emotional imbalance . . . or worse. Today they tell us that the role of the pet *is* that of surrogate child, and that we need have no guilt feelings about our deep emotional attachments, nor about our grief at the time of loss.

So, you see, there are differences of opinion, and the pendulum continues to swing toward extremes on both sides. The answers, no doubt, lie somewhere in the middle. (Wasn't it Shangri-La where moderation was the golden rule?) But at least there *is* a controversy, a discussion in the wind. The human/animal bond has finally been deemed worthy of serious study, and the results that are developing are fascinating.

Because children have been called "society's hope for the future," perhaps it is appropriate that we continue our review of the human/animal bond with them.

2.

In the Hands of Babes

Children and pets . . . a classic image. The two have been so closely associated in the mind's eye that they have become a beloved cliché around the world. The words are almost hyphenated—a boy-and-his-dog, a girl-and-her-horse. Some of the best-selling books, most-popular movies and highest-rated television programs of all time have concerned children and companion animals. I am pleased to report that even in our modern, supersonic society, the magic still works—the child/animal bond is alive and well and living in the most unlikely places.

A docent of the Los Angeles Zoo told me recently about one of her experiences with the Zoomobile, an outreach program that takes small animals, such as rabbits and guinea pigs, into inner-city schools. A rather rough-looking little boy of about seven swaggered up to her and, through clenched teeth, muttered, "Eh . . . you wanna see my switchblade?" At that moment he spotted the guinea pig in the woman's hands. His mouth fell open, the macho manner vanished, and a regular little seven-year-old cried, "Ooh . . . what's *that*?" The ice was broken, the bond was back.

The best way I know to describe what an animal can mean to a child is from the inside looking out. Thinking back to my own childhood, there were a legion of four-legged friends who helped me grow up. They had a job on their hands, too, not only with me but with the other two kids in the house, my mother and father, Tess and Horace.

Dad worked for an electronics firm all his life, and like Horatio Alger, Horace White rose from office boy to commercial vice-president. Somewhere in between (around "rookie salesman," I guess) came the Great Depression, and Dad built radio receivers at night to augment his income. Because few people had any extra cash, he began trading his goods and services for those of others.

It was inevitable that one day he swapped a radio for an adorable chow chow puppy. Mom was ecstatic and wasn't about to remind him that dogs eat more than crystal sets! Dad was on a roll, and before long there was a German shepherd, then two more chows . . . and soon he built our own little kennels in the backyard—with rotating house privileges for the guests, of course.

I believe we had as many as twenty-six of Dad's trade-offs at one time, but it wasn't destined to be the most successful dog business. Everyone was still short of money, a situation compounded by the fact that we got more emotionally involved with the dogs than we ever did with Dad's radios.

Then, too, the complications began to multiply when it turned out to be a worse than usual year for fleas—and they moved into the house along with the various privileged dogs. Not to worry. The ever-resourceful Horace had read somewhere that burning sulfur would get rid of every flea, so he proceeded to burn a pie tin of sulfur (try it—you won't like it!) in the middle of the living room. Unfortunately, he neglected to put something under the pan and burned a perfect little circle through our one nice rug to the floor beneath. Memory gets a little hazy at this point . . . something about not being able to afford a new rug *and* a divorce. . . . All I can remember is we gradually phased ourselves out of the kennel business. Suffice it to say, animalitis is hereditary.

Children are usually found in bunches. Even "only" children. While I had no brothers and sisters, there were always several "best friends" (two-legged) for company. I loved to play and race and scream with the rest, but there were times when being alone—particularly alone with animals—was my definite choice. I had been lucky enough to experience nature as a very small child, and I loved to explore quietly without the chattering of a peer group. Recently, Dr. Aaron Katcher was quoted as saying, "The speechless kind of companionship shared with pets may provide a sense of relaxation that humans, who demand talk as the price of companionship, may not provide." Maybe that's what was going on with me, and I didn't even know it.

From the time I was three years old, our summer vacations were spent packing into the High Sierras on horseback, with our supplies carried by a string of mules. The first year I rode with my dad, in front of him on the saddle, but the next year I graduated to a separate horse. In those days there were no ski lodges up there, no condos or paved highways. There were no roads at all, in fact, and our pack train would travel for two days over two passes, Glenn and Kearsarge, both about 12,000 feet in elevation. A guide would take us in to a magnificent area called Sixty Lake Basin, we'd set up camp, then guide, horses, and mules would head back to the ranch. We wouldn't see them—or anyone else—until they came in to get us two weeks later.

There was so much to investigate . . . chipmunks and black squirrels and magpies and deer . . . even an occasional bear . . . that the time just evaporated. My folks taught me just how much you can see if you are very still and let the animals get curious about *you*. Hard to imagine B.W. staying quiet that long, isn't it? Come to think of it, when I was a really small child, my mother even used that

ploy at home whenever she wanted me to take a nap.
"Let's pretend we are in the mountains. . . . See how still
you can lie and maybe the animals will come around. . . ."
I loved animals so much that I fell for this every time. Oh,
how I used to count the minutes all year long until it was
time to go back to the high country. Today, high camp is
something else entirely. . . .

Many things have indeed changed since I was a child,
some for the better, some for the worse. In the previous
chapter, I touched on what is considered by many to be one
of contemporary society's tragedies: the dissolution of so
many close-knit families. With modern technology changing our lives and livelihoods so rapidly, I would think that
people need to touch and be with each other now more
than ever. And perhaps children—who have never known
a quieter tone of life—need such togetherness even more
than the rest of us. Many of their favorite video games can
be a little like playing solitaire, to the extent that children
are interacting less, not only with their families but even
with each other.

How many families (even families of three) actually sit
down to breakfast together and discuss their plans for the
day? Sadly, not enough. Research indicates that each year
more and more students *from standard middle-class homes*
arrive at school without having eaten any breakfast at all.
Everyone in the household seems to have been left to "do
his own thing," and togetherness, even at meals, has been
lost in the shuffle.

This alienation . . . lack of companionship, according
to Dr. Boris Levinson, is modern man's number-one problem. He believes that many of the anxieties we experience
are partly due to our withdrawal "from the healing forces
of nature." Pets, particularly for a child, can reestablish
that link.

For example, pets allow youngsters to observe a more

natural rhythm of life than the one they usually see: Animals do not know the meaning of dieting; wild animals (without us to lead them astray) seldom overeat, they don't understand skipping a meal on purpose, and they know enough to rest when they are tired. The whole concept of "overachieving," of acquiring more and more and more, is almost totally foreign to the animal kingdom. (As with every rule, of course, there are exceptions: Jackdaws, shady relatives of our crows, have long been notorious for lining their nests with bright jewelry filched from the local gentry.)

On a larger scale, children often learn for the first time about life, death, reproduction, and biological processes by observing animals. Puppyhood through prime to old age and, ultimately, death—it's an overview of what we ourselves are experiencing at a slower rate.

Pets can help rebuild the bridge between human members of the family . . . between brother and sister, parent and child. Properly handled, a pet can be a "cooperation center," and discussions about the pet—his needs and antics—are activities in which everyone can participate.

Ann Cain, professor of psychiatric nursing at the University of Maryland, studied how family dynamics changed in some sixty households once a pet was introduced. She discovered that a number of the families experienced "increased closeness, more time playing together, and less arguing after they have gotten their pets." She cites one enterprising mother who used the family dog to quell arguments. "Stop fighting!" she'd say. "You're upsetting the dog!"

And they probably were.

A survey was conducted recently at the University of Minnesota, and one of the important conclusions, says Dr. Michael Robin, who headed the study, was that dogs and cats play an important part in the development of children, and supplement peer and parental relationships. The research team found that pets are "unconditionally" affectionate to children, and can be active physical playmates as well as "sources of comfort, companionship and responsibility."

The youths in Dr. Robin's study included teenagers in high schools, state correctional facilities, and psychiatric hospitals. Dr. Robin reported that 97 percent of those teens owning pets (of any and all varieties) said that they had liked or loved the animal very much, many considering it "a best friend" and "something to love." To quote Joan Arehart-Treichel, who summarized Dr. Robin's findings for *Science News* magazine, "In fact, for delinquents and emotionally disturbed youngsters, a pet had often been their sole love object. As one 18-year-old boy reported, 'My kitty was the joy of my life. It never hurt me or made me upset like my parents.'"

Sam and Elizabeth Corson, of Ohio State University's Department of Psychiatry, contend that dogs are particularly effective in providing comfort and companionship because of "their ability to offer love and tactile reassurance without criticism, and their maintenance is a sort of perpetual infantile dependence which may stimulate our natural tendency to offer support and protection."

Not everyone in the scientific community, however, is in total agreement on the child/animal bond. Dr. Aaron Katcher, though enthusiastic about the research being done, reminds us that it is too early to draw ironclad conclusions. "We have very little knowledge of the basic psychological effects of pet animals on child development. . . . We are just beginning to understand psychological effects of pets on individuals and vice versa."

Still, Dr. Levinson, who has been treating children with psychological problems for years, maintains that "the ownership of a pet may aid in the development of adaptive personality traits." Dr. Aline Kidd adds that pets can actually accelerate the learning process in children. "Experiencing animals as well as other children helps teach some of the happier as well as the more painful characteristics of life itself."

Pets have been found to be great teachers. Dr. Bruce Max Feldmann, director, University of California (Berkeley) Pet Center, notes, "Observing a pet's behavior may nurture assertiveness, independence, exploration, and self-confidence in a child." A youngster can also learn much from the responsibility of taking care of an animal. Dr. Levinson refers to this as giving the child a "feeling of mastery."

Many mothers and fathers today have jobs outside the home, and children often return from school to empty houses—these are the so-called "latch-key kids." When a child has a pet waiting, he not only has guaranteed companionship, but has certain duties to perform. A good example of early responsibility is the schedule shown here:

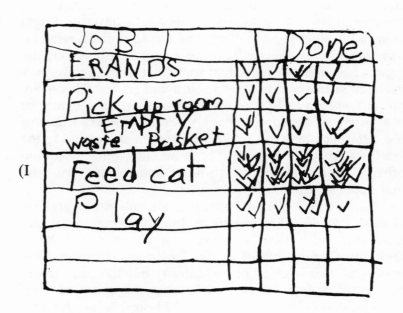

This was the way one eight-year-old boy, Jim, allocated his priorities. If you'll notice, there are more checks after feeding the cat than anywhere else, even after play. (I'd like to know him.) But even if a youngster is not as organized as our schedule keeper above, the very fact of "having a job to do" when coming home can foster a sense of self-esteem, especially when there is someone as obviously glad to see him as is the family pet.

Pets respond eagerly to care and attention and give children a socially acceptable outlet for *touching*. . . . There's that word again! They provide youngsters with a soft, cuddly object with which to develop tactile and sensory motor awareness.

A child is never too young to be taught *how* to touch, and that animals are not like stuffed toys but are living creatures that experience pain, thirst, and hunger, just as the child himself does. Gentle hands can be developed right along with walking and talking. As a child is discovering his own capabilities, he can be made aware of the varying degrees of strength he has—that there is a definite difference between strong-and-rough and firm-and-gentle. This is important when a child is touching any other living being, be it a puppy or kitten or a baby sister or brother. Knowing the difference between rough and gentle can be vital to the safety of the child himself if he is making contact with another creature larger and stronger than he is—one who may reply in kind.

Some children, of course, are not only not aggressive around animals—they fear them. Indeed, people of all ages have fears of various creatures. How a person handles these fears is very important. Dr. Levinson tells us that it is important that a child not withdraw, but face and try to overcome his fears. How well he does this can have a serious influence on his self-concept. Mastering his fear of a pet can improve his image of himself.

My great fear was of spiders. I was deathly afraid of them for most of my life. I still have to muster every ounce of self-control to escort a spider outside (which I do with an old peanut-butter jar)—and this is a relatively recent accomplishment . . . probably influenced by my reading *Charlotte's Web* about ten years ago. Prior to that, I had tried everything to overcome what was indeed a galloping phobia. As a teenager, I even let a big wolf spider stay in his web by the front door, thinking if I named him "George" and got to know him, I would get over my unreasonable fear. Well . . . for three months I went in and out of the back of the house, until "George" moved on and I could once again greet a date at the front door. We're talking *fear!*

Fear, of course, is contagious. If a parent expresses apprehension, a child will pick up on it right away . . . if only because the child normally looks to the parent for ultimate protection. Anything a parent fears is doubly threatening for the child. As a tot, if your mother cried, you automatically puckered up, too—even if you hadn't the foggiest idea what she was crying about.

Therefore, parents can set the example. If they seem to enjoy the pet, it will help the child enjoy it. Praising a youngster for his good interaction with animals will carry a lot more weight than all the don'ts in the world. Program the situation for success . . . allow the child some room for failure . . . don't give him too much responsibility to begin with . . . then congratulate him on the *right* choices he makes.

A young child beginning to communicate with pets will tend to talk *to,* rather than *down to,* an animal. This is not only because the child is a short person (and can make immediate eye contact) but because he hasn't yet learned to treat the animal as anything other than another intelligent being. (Such communication is more difficult for an adult, who may already have the built-in bad habit of talking down, even to the child.)

Many children, studies have found, come to identify with their pets. The two become peers, equals. A child often thinks his pet shares his feelings of sorrow, anger, joy, and this camaraderie allows the child to feel more secure. Indeed, some psychologists believe children identify more readily with animals than with other human beings. They can even communicate better with pets.

Being a pet's lord and master, being able to order him around, allows a child to be in command of a situation, and may make his own authority figures (his parents, teachers, older brothers and sisters) seem less overwhelming. Merely recognizing the fact that pets need to be trained, at least to some degree, helps a child accept and understand certain ground rules applied to himself.

Similarly, as a child develops a tolerance for his pet's mistakes, he may become more tolerant of his own difficulties in mastering all of his lessons. Carrying the reasoning one step forward, if the youngster can adjust his expectations of his pet to the needs of the animal, he may be better able to adjust himself to the needs of society later on.

The value of constancy and stability—touched on in Chapter One—cannot be stressed too much where children are concerned. Modern parents seem to want their children to be independent at an early age, but they don't always shore up that independence with the necessary emotional support.

A child and pet know they are mutually dependent. The child learns to give and take and share, and receives a portion of security in return. A child catches on very quickly to the fact that he does not have to "play a role" with his pet. He can merely be himself, and still rely on the pet to remain a faithful, noncompetitive friend. A child's association with a pet can, therefore, result in feelings of trust and confidence in another living creature.

Pauline Wallin, a family counselor, explains, "It's a whole lot easier entrusting your expression of affection with a dog than a person. A dog will love you whether you are tall or short, fat or thin, brilliant or dull, strong or weak. A pet's love and loyalty is unconditional, predictable, and nonjudgmental." Neither does it matter if Johnny or Mary flunked a test in school today, or if their rooms are in chaos—they still have a friend.

A pet offers a safe sounding board. Many times children feel emotions—such as love or tenderness—and are not able to express them. Pets help fill that gap. Aline Kidd points out that a pet's receptiveness is as important to teenagers as to small children: "I think of pets as being the 'security blankets' of adolescents. The girl who didn't get asked to the prom can tell her peers that she didn't really have time to go anyway, and then go home and cry with her pet. The boy who can't pass the driver's license test can explain his hatred for the examiner and plot a vengeance he'll never actually carry out to his dog or horse. The important thing in both cases is that the expression of feelings of anger or rejection to a companion animal makes it less likely that the adolescent will act out the feelings."

We have noted that modern families are much more mobile than those of previous generations. Writing in *A Nation of Strangers,* Vance Packard told us, "The average American moves about 14 times in his life" and "about 40 million Americans change their home address at least once every year." Packard goes on to suggest that "for an urban child under ten, a move of ten blocks throws him into a stranger environment than a move of twenty miles would for his parents."

Children may find this uprooting, with its accompanying fragmented friendships, a little easier to cope with if the family has one or more pets to assuage the initial loneliness. Again, the animals furnish a feeling of continuity between the old life and the new. As a bonus, pets can often open the way for making new friends in the new communities.

Mobility, unfortunately, is not the only disruptive element hitting modern lives; marital discord is another. Statistics show that 53 percent of all marriages end in divorce, and that many broken homes have children who become delinquent. The comfort given by a pet may keep the child from venting his frustrations in destructive acts.

With all these human problems to handle, it stands to reason that a pet is going to run out of steam now and again. Even sickness in animals—having to visit a doctor, eat a special diet, require rest, etc.—enables the child to equate these things with his own experiences. Observing his pets can convince a youngster of the relative nonseriousness of a few everyday maladies, as well. Nightmares, for instance, can be very scary. Dogs and even cats are known to have nightmares, and when a child learns he can soothe the animal with petting and comfort, he learns that an occasional bad dream is not so harmful.

The immutable fact is that the life-span of our companion animals is so much shorter than our own that we know right from the beginning that the day will come when we have to say good-bye. This is not to be morbidly dwelt upon, but rather to be considered an opportunity to understand our own life cycle. The actual death of a pet, then, can be a learning experience for the child, painful though it may be. It is, in a sense, something of a rehearsal for any later experiences he will have to face when human beings whom he loves die. It is his first encounter with something *nobody* can fix. I know it was for me. . . .

My constant buddy when I was around five or six years old was a dark red Pekingese, Chang, who took his job as my mentor very seriously, indeed. With the centuries-old patience of the Orient, he would tolerate my tea parties and still manage to maintain his dignity, sitting up opposite me at our toy table. It was about this time that a (two-legged) monster was prowling the neighborhoods, gaining attention by being known as the "Hollywood Dog Poisoner." His modus operandi was to throw fresh meat laced with ground glass into fenced-in yards. Ours, unfortunately, happened to be one of his random choices. This creature was finally caught, but not before I had to watch my beloved pal die . . . the hard way.

Tough as it was, my parents, themselves heartsick, did their best to answer all of my questions and explain away my anxieties.

The death of a pet is a child's first opportunity to appraise his own feelings about death and come to terms with them. Each young person will react differently, of course— some will bewail the loss, others grieve quietly; still others will hold a mock funeral and act out the feelings of mourning. Later, when a new animal comes along, the child learns that life goes on, and that there is yet another living pet who can love him and whom he can love.

I never heard what ultimately happened to the Hollywood Dog Poisoner, but I know that he was neither the first, nor the last, to exhibit such destructive behavior. Oddly enough, research has shown that some disturbed people can actually learn loving behavior from animals. A few years back, I attended a seminar and heard Dr. Wesley Young speaking on some of his experiences during years of veterinarian practice. He was, at one time, director of the Los Angeles Zoo. A boy had been caught mutilating some of the small animals in the children's section of the zoo, and he was arrested and brought to trial. As punishment the judge sentenced him to a period of time working in Dr. Young's veterinary hospital—with supervision, of course. This particular story has a happy ending, for ultimately the boy, after seeing animals being helped rather than harmed, opted to work toward a career as a veterinarian.

Thirteen-year-old Michelle Walters of Baltimore, Maryland, was spurred into action by a similar problem, and handled it in her own way. A lifelong animal lover, Michelle became incensed when she read that a couple of teenage boys had stoned to death some flamingos at her local zoo. She determined to write a book, to "show the world how nice animals are." She sent letters to all the prominent people in and around Baltimore, gathering animal anecdotes; wrote the book *Maryland Pet Profiles;* then sent out press releases to all the media telling what she'd done. Now she is a published author, who, at thirteen, warranted an interview on the *Today* show. When I heard her and called to congratulate her, she informed me that she was working on her second animal book. Talk about self-starters!

Before we close our chapter on pets and children, there are a few "precautionary" thoughts to be considered.

Parents should "planfully select" (a Levinson term) the right pet for their children. The doctor points out that "the pet is far too important and plays too great a role in the child's development for its choice to be left to mere chance."

It is very important to deal the child in when making that all-important choice of a pet. Surprises are wonderful, but not where a live animal is concerned. *Be sure* it is welcome. Research indicates that a child is much more inclined to love and care for a pet of his own choice than for one that has been foisted upon him. He will be much more co-operative if he feels he is *in* on the planning. Should the child's ideal pet be impractical, make sure he understands the reasons why, and work out a compromise.

Once a specific animal is under consideration, the new owners-to-be should learn as much about the animal as possible. Who were the pet's previous owners? What good or bad experiences has the animal had in the past? (All of this theorizing, mind you, is great if you are acquiring a pet on purpose. Sometimes the choice is taken completely out of your hands. Sooner, for example, was an unplanned blessing, and we had to adapt accordingly. I know nothing of the first several months of his life, and will *never* know what there is about heavy rain or thunder and lightning that makes him try to climb the walls.)

Once a pet has been adopted, it is vital to ease the

child, particularly a younger one, into his new life with an animal. Small children may feel pangs of rivalry, especially if the rest of the family is suddenly making the new addition the total center of attention. The same holds true if the family has another pet as well—be sure *everyone* is included in the new excitement and that they realize there is plenty of love to go around.

The child's activities with the new pet must, of course, be monitored. To expect a child to take over the *complete* care and feeding of a new pet is buying blue sky. Parents' responsibilities do not stop with bringing a new animal into the home. They must be aware of how that pet is being cared for, and guard against pet abuse. Sad but true, pet abuse, like child abuse, is widespread, and battered pets, like battered humans, are all too often undetectable by outsiders.

Just as tragic as battered pets are discarded or abandoned pets. Please do not bring a pet home if you do not plan to keep him. Every summer I hear the same sad stories about college students who kept pets all during the school year, but come June when it's time to go home, they simply leave the animals to fend for themselves. Just college-age immaturity? Unfortunately, no. Fully grown adults are known to go on vacation and take a puppy along for fun and games. Then, when it's time to return to the real world, the human/animal bond short-circuits and they leave Fido behind to take his chances. Many of these same people throw up their hands in horror over all the cruelty in the world!

When the situation is properly handled, then, there is still—even in our modern world—a strong affinity between pets and children. They still offer each other love and support. But just because an individual grows taller and older doesn't mean the animal/human connection is broken. Quite the contrary. Pets have a variety of jobs to take care of where we alleged adults are concerned. In fact, for many pets, the big jobs are just beginning.

3.

The Adult/Animal Bond

We seem to evaluate everything these days on a scale of one to ten . . . even our mortal health problems.

Heart disease is our number-one killer!

Cancer is number two!

Let's hear it for drunk driving!

It's almost as if it were a rating survey with everyone vying for the top spot.

The most serious disease in society today, however, is none of the above, according to Dr. James Lynch, professor of psychiatry, University of Maryland Medical School. He contends that *loneliness* is the true culprit, and that it has a direct bearing on all the others.

He says, "First, a great deal of research evidence indicates that long-term social isolation alters neurochemical and vascular processes in the body in such a way that it increases the susceptibility to major diseases. Second, loneliness brings on destructive behavior . . . increased smoking, drinking, and even suicide, for example."

What *is* loneliness? We keep hearing what it isn't— "loneliness isn't just being alone; one can be lonely in a crowd"—but we rarely hear a good definition of what it *is*. In her master's thesis, Judy Harris of Sepulveda, California, has come as close as anyone I've read: "Loneliness is not not knowing others; it is not being known by others."

Mrs. Harris points out that in one day we come into contact with more people than our ancestors did in a lifetime. As a result, our "processes of attachment are accelerating, making it more and more difficult to develop meaningful relationships."

This seems obvious once it is said, but how many of us stop long enough to think about it? Take a minute right now to list the people with whom you can risk total honesty, with whom you can just be *you*. Personally, the people who really know me, and with whom I am completely myself, are few . . . and for the most part four-legged.

According to Dr. Aline Kidd, "A companion-animal, a pet, may have a positive effect on an interpersonal relationship." A recent five-year study, conducted by Johns Hopkins in conjunction with the national Institute on Aging, concerned the health problems of bereavement. As writer Gail Fillmore explains, "The people studied were widows, and one of the findings was that women who had felt close relationships with their pets were also more likely to have had close relationships with their husbands."

Allen, when we met, was a widower with three children: David, fourteen, Martha, thirteen, and Sarah, ten . . . and two miniature chocolate poodles, Willie and Emma, ten months old. Allen had bought the puppies, littermates, after the children's mother had died the year before. He always credited them with clinching our courtship, since it took me a whole year to get smart and say yes.

The loss of a loved one is, of course, something we must all face sooner or later. Allen knew that bringing Willie and Emma into the house would help his children overcome their mother's death, and I've already mentioned how our pets helped me through the painful months after Allen's own death. Dr. Aaron Katcher, addressing the potential health values of pet ownership, indicates, "The loss of a spouse is accompanied by an increase in the frequency of illness and an increase in death rate during the first one or two years after bereavement." He adds, "There is abundant evidence to suggest that the companionship provided by pets has the capacity to both reduce the frequency of serious disease and prolong life."

Pet owning, therefore, can be thought of as preventive medicine for those of us everyday, so-called normal adults.

No less than they do with children, pets provide grown-ups with a source of security, increased communication, amusement, friendly intimacy, companionship, and, as Freud defined it, "affection without ambivalence."

A universal effort is being made to gather specific scientific documentation on a subject that has long been rife with emotion and theoretical speculation.

Documenting tangible evidence of anything as subjective as the feeling between pets and people means compiling astronomical numbers of case histories for comparison. I will leave the aggregate for the professionals and concentrate on individuals.

At some time or other almost everyone has noticed a great similarity between a person and his or her pet. News cameramen revel in finding these look-alikes whenever they are covering a dog show.

Dr. Michael Fox, in his *Pet Owner Relations,* gives us reason to believe that possibly these similarities stem from our own personalities. He says, "More independent 'inner-directed' people will keep a cat in preference to a dog simply for its aesthetic qualities and its less demanding attitude. . . . An insecure or paranoid person may want a powerful guard dog. Another person who is attempting to live up to an ego image of grace and agility may keep an Afghan hound or a Saluki."

Not everyone fits the mold. A universal image of grace

and agility is Fred Astaire. Does Fred have a Saluki or an Afghan? No, but he had a rabbit he was crazy about!

Rather recently, Fred married Robyn Smith, who had been one of the few women jockeys in the country. A mutual interest in horses was to be expected—Fred had raised Thoroughbreds for years—but Robyn brought along her own version of the human/animal bond. Fred admits he never expected his household to include ducks and chickens and a rabbit, much less that he would enjoy it. They both grew very fond of the rabbit, Thumper. Reportedly housebroken, he was given free run of the house and would follow Robyn around and wait at her door to be let in to play. Fred described the affectionate response they received from this little fellow, and both were teary-eyed when they ultimately had to tell me that Thumper had disappeared in the garden one day, victim of some creature larger and less gentle than himself.

One ideal example of the classic adult human/animal bond would have to be that between John Steinbeck and his Charley.

Charley was a standard French poodle. *French* because he came from France, you see, and while he eventually learned broken English, he would respond instantly only if addressed in his native French. Woe betide anyone who talked cutesy dog talk to Charley—if he didn't nail you, John would. They were each one of a kind and thank God they found each other.

At one point in his life, around 1960, Steinbeck felt strongly that it was time to reacquaint himself with the land he wrote about so intimately . . . by driving through it instead of flying above it. He determined to leave behind him his celebrity identity, and even the company of his beloved wife, Elaine; he would take three months for the journey

. . . alone. But not quite. As a hedge against loneliness, he took along his friend, Charles le Chien, because, in Steinbeck's own words, "A dog, particularly an exotic like Charley, is a bond between strangers."

If you have read *Travels with Charley,* you are lucky to know something already of the unique rapport that was theirs.

I was even luckier.

Allen had been friends with the Steinbecks for many years, since Allen and Elaine had attended the University of Texas together and had remained close buddies ever since. When I came into the picture, one of the first things Allen did was take me to John and Elaine's New York home to meet them. (Or to get their stamp of approval perhaps.) All I know is, mine was the worst case of stage fright in history. I was newly in love, which does nothing for one's poise, and I was being taken to meet The Legend . . . who, at the precise moment we walked in was scratching out his acceptance speech for the Nobel Prize. The usual brief introductions immediately gave way to Steinbeck's asking us if we could think of a synonym he was fishing for to replace a certain word. This didn't help my state of nerves one bit . . . John Steinbeck asking *us* for a synonym when I couldn't think of my name! To this day I cannot remember what word he was trying to replace.

It was about this time that Charley decided to grace us with his presence. He didn't trot into the room . . . he entered. He took in the entire scene with one appraising glance and advanced to John, then Elaine, who explained that Charley wasn't being rude, he simply didn't make up to strangers. I had read *Travels with Charley* very recently and I couldn't take my eyes off this tall grizzled dog. I kept my hand out and available in case he should brush by, while he simply stared back at me as the conversation went on around him. Finally—with what could only be interpreted as a Gallic shrug—he came over, laid his rough head on my lap, and settled down to stay. That took care of the stage fright.

When I got home later that night, I discovered that Charley had gotten some mud on my black chiffon skirt. I carefully folded the skirt and put it away where it remains to this day. Elaine and John used to tease me about that, but how many perfect evenings are there in a lifetime?

"There are two kinds of people . . . those who love animals and those who hate people who love animals!" So says Dr. Alan Beck, associate professor of animal ecology, University of Pennsylvania. A word to the wise: It is better not to force the issue, lest you polarize an animal disliker into an animal *hater*.

Pablo Casals saw it another way. He said, "There are, I know, people who do not love animals, but I think this is because they do not understand them . . . or because, indeed, they do not really see them. . . . I find in them a longing to communicate and a real capacity for love. If sometimes they do not trust but fear man, it is because he has treated them with arrogance and insensitivity."

There are some people who simply don't *like* pets. Fair enough. I have respect for those who are frank about telling me up front that animals turn them off . . . rather than trying to pretend otherwise. One needs only to watch a person's hands on an animal to get the true picture.

When I first started dating, I went out a few times with a fellow who made a great show of how crazy he was about animals. He'd come on very strong with our dogs (a Peke, a poodle, and a St. Bernard) and must have grated on them as much as he did on me; he didn't get to first base with any of us, and I had to tell him I didn't want to see him anymore. This happened right before Easter, and sure enough, come Easter morning there was a tiny live white bunny in a basket at my front door from you-know-who. Big animal lover that he was, he had missed the point entirely that I did not approve of live pets as Easter gifts. Or maybe *I* missed the point. That adorable bunny turned out to be a real savage . . . the only one I've ever seen that wouldn't gentle down in spite of my most patient efforts. My ex-friend must have searched far and wide to find the only attack rabbit in existence. I finally had to give up and place the little devil on a ranch with a lot of other rabbits. *He* knew what he was doing!

Even pet-*loving* adults, as well as children, can be overly impulsive in acquiring a pet. They fall in love too easily with little regard for what may lie ahead. In getting a pet, it might be well to look at a few valid considerations:

Personal Life-style. There is no denying that having a pet means assuming a certain commitment of time. Spur-of-the-moment plans to spend the evening—or the night—out may sound like great fun, but it can be frustrating and uncomfortable for the animal waiting at home. No matter how understanding he may be, an animal's body clock is on a fairly regular schedule, and to avoid problems it is best to feed him and let him out at approximately the same time every day. He's more than willing to compromise, but it might take a little planning ahead.

The same holds true when making travel plans. Be sure to remember that since he's a card-carrying member of your family, arrangements must be made for the pet in your life too. See that he will be cared for in your absence, or take him along. Whichever, check out the situation—the less left to chance, the better.

Allergies. Some people are allergic, in varying degrees, to animal dander. This can range from mild irritation to very serious health problems. Statistics have shown that among those who have been told by their doctors that they should get rid of the family pet to alleviate their discomfort, three out of four have chosen to keep the animal. In severe cases, however, don't press your luck.

Housing Limitations. As we mentioned, when looking for a place to live these days, "no pets" can be a familiar song. Sad to say, much of this has been brought on by the pet owners themselves. Bad pet manners are a real turnoff to everyone, especially those who aren't animal-oriented in the first place, and the real fault lies at the human end of the leash. A relatively few unthinking people have ruined it for the rest, who maintain supervision over their pets out of consideration for property and the rights of others.

On the drawing board are plans for some future multiple dwellings specifically designed to allow pets to live there, too, without interfering with neighbors' privacy. Similar plans will help an even more pressing priority, as the number of "no children" signs continue to multiply. As of this writing, there is still no immediate substitute for personal responsibility.

I have no room to talk. Some years back (a euphemism) I was married to a very nice man, Lane Allan. As a wedding present, he surprised me with an adorable eight-week-old Pekingese puppy . . . the ultimate gift as far as I was concerned. My growing-up years had always included Pekes in the family, and they are all anyone could wish for in a pet: brave, funny, hardy, loving, and oh, so smart.

Well, we named this little fellow Bandit, and from the first moment he was put in my arms we were committed to each other. There was one complication—Lane had lived for several years in Park La Brea, an apartment complex in Los Angeles. When the time came for the bride and the new little one to move in, we suddenly discovered there was a stringent no-pet rule.

Now, all my life I have had a deep respect for law and order. Put up any sign and I'll obey it. I don't run in the halls, or step on the grass, and I will wait forever for the WALK sign at a corner. Put to the test, however, and confronted by a rule I couldn't live with, my integrity went to hell in a handbasket. We couldn't afford to move, and the puppy was not about to be displaced.

"No problem," she cried. "I can handle this tiny fellow and no one will be any the wiser!"

Remember . . . do as I *say,* not as I do.

Paper-training Bandy was easy, and he accompanied us everywhere so he was never left alone in the apartment in case he'd cry and blow the cover. We also had a park nearby where we would have some good daily walks. To smuggle him in and out of the apartment, I would hide him under my coat. He caught on to this game very quickly, so that whenever he saw the coat he would begin to dance and carry on, but the minute I picked him up he would go limp and still as a stuffed toy. He was a terrific co-conspirator.

As time went by there was a growing difficulty. Literally. He kept growing. Not just to adult size—he went past that. He grew into the most beautiful, but the *biggest* Peke I have ever known. We called him our Standard Pekingese. Another thing—this had all started in November, and by now the winter months had passed into spring, which was rapidly turning into a sunny, warm California summer.

Have you ever tried to look nonchalant walking out of your house wearing shorts and carrying a heavy—and I mean *heavy*—coat over your arm? I also had to keep a sharp eye out for the security guards who patrolled the area. We would nod and smile, but I never lingered for conversation as I could feel my little bundle tensing up to join in.

I can't remember how many times we acted out this charade before the inevitable happened. One morning as I was making my getaway, one of the security men called after me. "Mrs. Allan, you'd better check that coat! It keeps wagging its tail!"

Caught flatfooted, what could I say? But he couldn't have been nicer. He said they had been aware of my stowaway for some time, and as long as I kept my secret from the other residents, they would continue to play my game.

And they did . . . for two whole years until Bandy and I moved out.

The John Steinbecks and Allen Luddens were supremely fortunate to enjoy that elusive commodity . . . a happy marriage.

Many marriage situations, unfortunately, are less than ideal, and where there are no children involved to constitute a buffer zone, a pet may be one of the few safe subjects of conversation—or if not safe, at least an excuse to reopen lines of communication.

A pet, especially a dog or cat, is often involved as a substitute in an emotionally unfulfilling relationship. In a childless marriage, for example, the pet can act as the surrogate child. This is also true both before the children arrive and after they have flown the coop.

In the former case, some psychologists feel that learning to cope with the demands of a puppy or kitten can help a young couple resolve some of their mixed feelings about introducing a baby on the scene. Being able to enjoy a pet while having to do some of the more disagreeable tasks that are inevitable prepares the prospective parents for enjoying the baby even while handling the less romantic work entailed.

In the latter circumstance—in which the children have grown and moved on—parents often find that animals fill the need to be needed. According to Dr. Bruce Max Feldmann, "Allowing pet owners to love and feel loved may be the greatest contribution made by pets to mental health and emotional well-being."

It is sad but true that fewer than half of today's marriages work. Dr. Lynch feels that some people place too much emphasis on marriage. "They are expecting too much from that one relationship. I cannot believe that one human being is capable of completely fulfilling another's needs."

Because pets do sometimes serve as surrogate children, if such a marriage breaks up, an animal can find himself being used as a pawn in a divorce situation. The pet becomes a bone of contention between two warring factions . . . and this has been known to be carried to rather unpleasant extremes. In one bitter contest, when the husband sued for divorce, the wife refused to settle until she was granted visiting rights to see the dogs. Even worse, there was the case of a wife so intent on revenge against her estranged husband that she took his two German shepherds to be euthanized. Fortunately, the veterinarian stalled until the husband could come and rescue his dogs.

When there actually *is* a child involved in a divorce action, he is in for an extremely traumatic experience, torn by his love for both parents. A pet can help such a child by bearing the brunt of his emotional conflict and providing acceptance and affection.

Suppose this upheaval is compounded once more by the remarriage of one or both parents? The youngster can *still* adjust to his new situation with some sense of stability and continuity in the realization that his four-footed friend has stuck with him.

Breaking up any marriage is a painful experience at best. Even when the two main characters try to be as grown-up and considerate of each other as possible, it still leaves a sense of failure and disorientation.

In Lane's and my case, letting me have custody of Bandit was a real sacrifice on Lane's part, as he loved the little guy as much as I did.

About two years after we split up, Lane stopped by to see me one day while I was working. I was doing a little half-hour talk show in which I answered letters from viewers and sang a couple of songs. I had brought Bandy on for the first show a while back, and he took to the camera like he was born to the cloth, so there was nothing for it but to make him a permanent member of the cast; he would lie quietly at my feet for the whole half hour.

We broadcast from the stage of what had been a small neighborhood movie theater converted for television; with no studio audience, the back of the theater where the seats were was dark and empty.

On this particular day, as we were signing off the show, Bandit began wagging his tail furiously, then took off up the aisle into the back of the house . . . something he had never done. As it turned out, Lane had been watching the show, then had stood up as the show ended to come up to where we were. Bandy, always very remote with strangers, had spotted that familiar outline in the dark, that far away, and after two years! *I* hadn't known who it was until Lane had stepped into the light. Bandy was all over him, kissing and whimpering hysterically. It was too much for us, and we three had a good cry together, which almost changed the course of our futures.

Almost . . .

Getting together can sometimes be as awkward for two people as breaking up, and pets have been found to be great matchmakers. A Los Angeles woman has recently caught on to the "common interest" benefit pets can provide for strangers, and has started a new singles dating service for animal lovers only. The group, reportedly more than two hundred strong, is comprised primarily of singles-with-pets who wish to meet—and possibly get serious about—other animal lovers. The group was started by people who apparently had had bad experiences with girl- and boyfriends who did not appreciate having a pet around. Gaining momentum, this new service tries to circumvent such disappointments. Once again, pets are running interference . . . even in the game of boy meets girl.

As we continue to study the pet/people relationships in our daily lives, it might be well to consider the effects this bonding may have on the four-legged half of our team. How is *he* reacting?

As we lean more and more heavily on our domesticated animals to provide us with a link to nature in our stressful modern existence, we may be imposing some of our neuroses on them as well. If we admit to having difficulty adjusting to changes that have catapulted us from the discovery of the wheel to the computer in a comparatively short period of time . . . consider our friend the dog. He is not only having to cope with some of the same situations that are driving us bananas but he finds that in the interim he has been remodeled into hundreds of disparate shapes and sizes to conform with our needs and fancies. It is hard to realize that St. Bernard and Pekingese, sheep dog and Mexican Hairless, are all the same animal. Dogs have *earned* a neurosis or two.

As tuned in to our moods as they are, it stands to reason that dogs—and to some extent, cats too—would reflect the same tensions that are sending us up the wall. Veterinarians, worldwide, are reporting more cases of neurotic animals with psychosomatic illnesses than ever before. Mentally disturbed—not to the point of being vicious except in extreme cases—just pretty well mixed up.

Veterinarians are becoming aware that some of their clients bringing in "sick" pets, are, in fact, mirroring their own illnesses. Anxious owners will tend to have anxious pets. Overweight owners will often have overfed pets. Human phobias can be like a virulent disease to dogs. We know they take their cues from our voices, our facial expressions, our body language. If we are fidgety, they tend to be jumpy. If our voices are raised in anger having nothing to do with them . . . they will echo the upset.

The physical health of our companion animals is improving, and their life-span is increasing, but so is the incidence of nervous ailments. There is a burgeoning group of animal psychiatrists and psychologists being kept very busy with a clientele made up of dogs and cats.

In *Wild Heritage* Sally Carrigher said, "Insanity is a human development. We have accepted senselessness as a kind of mad norm . . . animals couldn't stand such disorder. So far as we know, animals in the wild do not have mental illness. Except for brain injuries or *disease,* they are sane."

There was a study completed in West Germany that struck a little close to home with me. People who let their pets watch television more than an hour a day are risking the animals' well-being. Poodles, for example, who viewed TV for three to four hours a day became nervous or snappy and suffered acute loss of appetite. (Couldn't they at least have tested some other breed, Timmy?) The effect on birds is worse. After being subjected to several hours of TV daily, parakeets came down with fever. Among the pets studied, dogs were the most avid TV fans. Obviously, television is not for the birds.

So while the pets we look to for surcease from our problems are making us feel better . . . we may be making them feel worse. As happens with good friends, our tendency is to impose on them. But *good* friends keep coming back for more. Suffice it to say, our companion animals contribute a great deal to the quality of life.

Let's move on to see what the human/animal bond means to people to whom "quality of life" takes on a whole new meaning.

Allen always said that acting on television is only a hobby for me—animals, like
Willie and Nicky here, are my real vocation.

Animals were always a way of life around our house, especially after Dad started trading his radios for little guys like this chow-chow.

But even at age five, my best buddy was Chang, a sweet wine-red Pekingese.

Carefully posed by a photographer, this was supposed to look casual . . . but Bandit blew the cover. (That's Captain, our Great Pyrenees, on the wall.)

Stormy was confused as to just who should be the lap dog.

Bandy and I felt comfortable posing by our front door. George, the spider, had long since moved on.

A thirty-year friendship started when Ralph Helfer brought his macaws to appear on my first television series. . . .

Years later, Chuck Eisenmann's multitalented German shepherds, Venus, Hobo, London, and Raura, appeared on *The Pet Set*.

4.

We're Never Too Old

Perhaps no aspect of the human/animal bond is more important than that between pets and the elderly . . . if for no other reason than that old age is a state that sooner or later will affect us all.

Census statistics indicate that the size of the world's population over sixty-five years of age is growing every day, both in absolute numbers and in percentage of the whole.

Moreover, at least until recently, our society has been sorely lacking in programs that boost both the image and importance of the elderly. We are very youth-oriented, and everything from our entertainments to our advertising reflects this. What happens, then, when an individual who has been exposed to such intense youth orientation all his life reaches retirement age? According to Dr. Paula Gray, activity director at New York City's Jewish Home and Hospital for the Aged, many of her clients are hampered by the negative attitudes toward aging that they formed early in their lives. It's the old "nobody loves you when you're old and gray" routine, and in many instances, this becomes a self-fulfilling prophecy.

Fortunately, there has been a general shakeup in attitudes toward the elderly of late, and high time!

Many elderly people have discovered that pets satisfy

their greatest needs and trigger a reversal of many of the negative self-images. According to Dr. Leo Bustad, "Pets restore order to their basic lives; provide a more secure grasp of reality; and link their owners to a community of caring, concern, sacrifice, and intense emotional relationships." We "little old ladies in tennis shoes" are in on a good thing.

By current estimates, 22.5 million Americans are sixty-five years of age or older . . . one fifth of that number are over eighty. It has been estimated that by the year 2000, the number of those over eighty will reach 6 million. The current number of people over sixty-five is expected to more than double by the year 2030, rising to include more than 50 million people, or 17 percent of the total population.

These aren't just statistics . . . these numbers are *us*!

The numbers alone, however, may not mean so much, at least until one considers the ramifications—the cost of health care, for instance. Because the demand for care rises with age, the cost of health services will be increased dramatically, and they will be borne by relatively fewer people (those left in the work force). It behooves us all, then, to investigate any and all possible cost-saving avenues that may reduce the need for health care and enrich the lives of the elderly.

There is preliminary evidence, documented by Dr. Aaron Katcher and Dr. Erika Friedmann in their 1980 study of coronary patients, that companion animals may allow the elderly to live longer, healthier lives. To quote Dr. Katcher, "Pet ownership was significantly associated with a lower death rate. The positive effect of pets was not limited to dog owners (dogs being the type of pets which provide a stimulus to exercise). It is extremely important to recognize that there are no data which indicate that dogs or cats influence health or morale more favorably than birds, horses, small mammals, or even fish or lizards."

Approximately 95 percent of our elderly live at home (as opposed to in an institution), and most of the advantages to owning a pet, as outlined in earlier chapters, apply. Sometimes to an even greater degree. Pets have been found to decrease loneliness in the elderly, give a person something to care for, something to watch and perhaps play with, something that provides a sense of security, something that stimulates some degree of exercise . . . above all, something that necessitates maintaining some kind of daily routine: A canary or parakeet will be up and chirping every morning, a dog will need to go out, a cat will insist on being fed . . . none of them will take no for an answer.

Loneliness, of course, can—and does—affect young and old alike. But the elderly seem particularly susceptible, thanks to the conventions of modern society. Elderly people, for the most part, have retired from their jobs and often have lost day-to-day contact with their children. Many are widows or widowers, and literally live alone. Irene M. Burnside, a gerontological nurse and author, points out that the loneliness experienced by the elderly may result in feelings of "emotional isolation," of being locked in one's self and unable to obtain warmth and comfort from others.

Dorothy Walster, of the Scottish Health Education Unit in Edinburgh, states, "The overall picture of loneliness and rejection in the western world, with its emphasis on youth, has a disastrous effect on the mental health of the elderly—and can be greatly alleviated by pet ownership."

It is in the most developed countries that a pet as the last link with life for an elderly person is most often found

. . . a contrast to the agricultural communities of the Third World, where elders remain as members of the family unit. "Pets are a source of ongoing life," says author Patricia Curtis. "They serve as a much-needed connection to youth. . . . A pet is the greatest ego booster in the world, they think you're the greatest!"

Pets ease the advent of old age by diverting an older person's attention *away from himself* and onto the playful antics of a dog or cat. The aches and pains are momentarily forgotten.

Retirement, of course, can be one of life's greatest traumas for many people. There used to be a saying, "You are what you eat," but in reality, we tend to define ourselves by our jobs—"we are what we *do*." Our work is often the source of our self-definition and self-satisfaction. "As a worker, you have a sense of belonging to the producing part of society," says behavioral scientist Leland P. Bradford. "Work helps to give you an identity. It is a source of human contact. It defines your goals and gives you a sense of accomplishment and affirmation."

To have this work ethic suddenly come to a halt can be a shock.

Some of the most difficult adjustments for the elderly today happen when they cease to be *producers*. The actuarial tables of any insurance company can offer telltale statistics on the number of people, men in particular, who die at or around the age of sixty-five—mandatory retirement age. All work and no play make Jack not only dull, but a prime candidate for monumental depression when his "all work" stops.

Pets can bring new dimensions to an older person's life, particularly to one who has lost intimate human companions and feels deserted by society. Having to care for an animal gives many a sense of being useful again, being needed. To many a senior citizen, the pet is the one confidant he has who realizes he is still an identifiable person. With the animal he is free to relax and be himself without fear of rejection or correction. He is provider, caretaker, and decision maker for his pet . . . as he was earlier in life. This fosters a feeling of independence, even when everything else is being done *for him.* Many choose against suicide solely for fear of the fate of their pet.

"If activity is a keynote to health," says Dorothy Walster, "there is no end to the ways that a pet can provide the means of activity."

Pets, particularly dogs, have been found to instill in many people, especially the elderly, a sense of safety and security. As Dr. Katcher explains, "For the urban elderly, crime in the streets is a personal experience rather than a political slogan. . . . A dog can decrease fear and make a home neighborhood feel safer, thereby increasing the willingness of the elderly to move about." It does not need to be a large dog, which might be more difficult for an older person to handle; a small dog is just as effective. One doesn't need an attack weapon, simply an early-warning system.

The pet may thus become the center of a retiree's life. People who once lived totally for their jobs (or even for their now-grown children) now may channel their energies toward their animals. Enterprising souls have even been known to embark on whole new careers, breeding or even speaking about pets. There is an organization in Los Angeles made up of senior citizens who hire out as pet-sitters. Unable to own a pet themselves, but still hungry to be around animals, they can enjoy being hired to come and stay with a dog or a bird in his own home while his people are away . . . and make a little income at the same time.

*   *   *

As a person grows older, his circle of friends may diminish, as individuals die or move away, says Dr. Levinson. A dwindling number of friends can result in increased feelings of alienation. A pet, the doctor says, may serve to "enhance one's relationships in the community. Neighbors may meet when walking their dogs . . . and the dog serves as the common denominator, thus making it possible for new interests and friendships to rise."

Going hand in hand with this is a pet's ability to prompt one to reminisce. Scientists are discovering such trips down memory lane to be very therapeutic. They not only keep a person in contact with his past (and his self-image), they reinforce the present, and keep one in tune with reality. In addition, reminiscences are known to be, in themselves, relaxing and soothing.

A few generations ago, before newspapers and radio and television—and before the lines between the generations were so rigidly drawn—the reminiscences of the old were a way of learning for the young. Our children are better *educated* today, but their general knowledge for the most part is pretty spotty. There is a disturbing tendency in even the very young to slam an interesting door with, "That was before my time." A pet, on the contrary, will listen to the same story again and again.

Animals other than dogs and cats—farm animals—are especially effective in evoking those early memories that are found to be so beneficial. Dr. Bustad told me of one program that used a lamb as a therapeutic pet. The little fellow proved of immeasurable help to these particular patients, many of whom had been sheepherders. When the time came for the lamb—now a sheep—to be sold, he was bought and presented back as a gift. In the course of conversation, Dr. Bustad volunteered that *his* favorite animals are goats, as they relate so easily to humans.

Touching, as we have stressed before, is very important . . . perhaps even more so for the elderly, considering
their more isolated life-styles. The sense of touch can diminish along with the other four senses . . . simply through
lack of use. As the *need* to touch someone . . . something
. . . increases, the opportunities for that touching are less
frequent. In tests conducted at the Florida Institute University in Miami, of dog/people interactions, *hand contact*
(rubbing, scratching, patting, or stroking) was most preva-
lent—among men as well as women. The indication was
that dogs provide a socially acceptable outlet for touching
. . . something that American men are reluctant to en-
gage in.

Dr. Michael McCulloch points out that the physical de-
terioration which occurs in old age can also result in depression. Pets, he says, can alleviate this, thanks to their
ability to provide companionship and to make us laugh.
And Dr. Bustad agrees: "More and more we are coming to
realize that it's very healthy to laugh, to dissolve our cares
and self-concern momentarily in the joyous surrender of
laughter. . . . The physiological and psychological benefits
from laughter, with its resultant lessening of tension,
should not be underestimated."

There is a quote I love from the Koran: "He deserves
Paradise who makes his companions laugh." In virtually
every evaluation of animals used as therapeutic assistants,
or even in describing their value as household pets, "adds
humor" is near the top of the list.

Dr. Bustad has been a pioneer in involving the veterinary students at Washington State University (also working
with the University of Idaho) in innovative projects that
allow the elderly to benefit from contact with companion
animals. Washington State has received a grant from
SAFECO, an insurance company, to develop guidelines for

placement of pets with the institutionalized elderly. People who may not necessarily want (or be able to keep) a pet of their own can serve as volunteers in the local therapeutic-riding program. Older volunteers also assist in taking small animals into the public schools for "show and tell" sessions.

There are also various groups around the country working to bring pets and the elderly together at home. CATS—Children and Animals Together for Seniors—is a federally and privately funded program headquartered in New York City that provides pets for the elderly. It also provides free food, medical care, and services. Founded in 1979 by actress Judith Feldman, CATS teams dogs and cats from the Bide-a-Wee animal shelters (and private individuals) with elderly who are lonely or shut-ins.

Miss Feldman explains, "I learned from veterinarians, psychiatrists, animal trainers and fanciers and films that uniting animals with older, isolated, institutionalized people brought meaning, renewed vigor and happiness to all concerned, including the animals. This knowledge sparked in me an increased determination . . . to match these folks with loving pets *before* they became institutionalized, to keep these people in society, in their own homes, surrounded by familiar things and neighborhood people, relatives who would no longer view them with disdain or treat them as excess baggage."

Augmenting the people/pet partnerships in CATS is a young/old liaison involving volunteers from local Girl Scouts, Boy Scouts, 4-H Clubs, high schools, and junior high schools, who assist in training the pets before they are placed and walking them after they are in their new homes.

PACT—People and Animals Coming Together—is a similar, volunteer nonprofit organization affiliated with the Gerontology Center of Pennsylvania State University. Its purpose, however, is twofold: Like CATS, it serves to pro-

mote and support pet ownership by older persons in the
community, but also—and this is especially important—it
is conducting longitudinal research to *measure* the effect of
pet ownership on the health and well-being of a sample of
rural elderly people. (Such documented studies are sorely
needed for society's overall acceptance of the benefits of
the human/animal bond.)

PACT's leaders, Dr. Dan Lago, Barbara Knight, and
Cathleen Cornell, indicate that their work has already
come face to face with a few long-standing prejudices:
"Some people feel it is immoral to consider spending resources on pet animals while human beings have unmet
needs. . . . Such opposition to PACT, and similar programs, is based on a view of the world that only humans,
and not animals, have significant moral standing."

Such ideas, of course, miss the point. They overlook
the whole notion that animals can make a valuable contribution to human welfare. As Lago and his associates state,
"Companion animals serve as direct and immediate re-
minders that we humans are not in the world alone, but
share space and responsibilities with other organisms in a
larger ecological totality."

In short: Hey, fellas, we're all on this planet together. . . . Let's help *each other* out!

And that's just what PACT is trying to do, by carefully
matching pets with elderly people seeking companion animals. "It is important," say Dr. Lago et al., "that the potential client have a strong personal desire to have a pet.
The client should have the physical ability to provide a
good deal of the pet's daily care needs. . . . It has not been
necessary to refuse many clients; even severely impaired
persons have been able to own animals."

PACT makes every effort to seek out any desired con-
ventional pet, and dogs have proven to be the overwhelming favorite. The program has a firm policy that any and all

placements are returnable, which minimizes the dangers of a mismatch and also assures the owners that animals will be cared for should they themselves die or become incapacitated.

The Carroll County Humane Society in Westminster, Maryland, also places pets with elderly people in their own homes and, like PACT, does so using special care and precautions. Project director Sheila McNamara generally recommends, for instance, that older adopters choose mature adult dogs rather than frisky puppies. She indicates that many of her clients prefer smaller dogs that have been spayed or neutered.

In Oregon, the Humane Society of Willamette Valley underscores the relative importance of more mature dogs for the elderly in its publication *Brief Paws*. "From a practical standpoint, the older pet can often make the better pet. The pet usually has had some training, is completely housebroken, has outgrown the chewing and climbing habits of a younger pet, and has settled into a more quiet lifestyle." May I add that gratitude from the animals is a very real bonus. They've been around, and often know a good thing when they find it.

Susan Bury Stauffer, former editor of *Shelter Sense,* the official publication of the Humane Society of the United States, indicates that there are also many organizations trying to make life easier for those elderly people who already own a pet. She states, for example, that places like Fort Wayne, Indiana; Palm Beach, Florida; Albuquerque, New Mexico; and Multnomah County, Oregon, have reduced fees for pet licenses or pet-neutering surgery for owners sixty-five and older.

Ms. Stauffer also commends:

• The Mobile, Alabama, SPCA, which helps the elderly by transporting their pets to veterinarians.

• The Humane Society of Missouri in St. Louis, which raised money to buy food for pets belonging to the elderly in need.
• The Morris County (New Jersey) Welfare Department, which boarded the pets of elderly people who had to be given temporary housing when they could not pay their heating bills.
• The Animal Medical Center in New York City, which offers free medical care for pets belonging to the elderly or those on limited incomes.

There are also several cities with mobile-unit veterinary care. In some instances this service makes the difference between possible and impossible pet ownership, particularly in the senior-citizen community.

Dr. Stephen Kritsick, director of emergency service at New York's Animal Medical Center, told Ms. Stauffer that the elderly often make better pet owners than younger adults who are away at work all day. It is out of consideration for the pet, however, that many elderly people are reluctant to adopt a companion animal. They worry about what will happen to the pet if they themselves die. This is a real concern, especially for folks who do not have family or friends willing to adopt the displaced pet. New ideas are needed here, and a few like PACT's are being actualized. The People-Pet Partnership staff at Washington State, for instance, has set up a foster care program for "survivor" pets.

While many elderly worry about what will happen to the pet if they die first, others dread the day the pet itself dies and leaves them with a huge gap in their lives. Dr. Aaron Katcher agrees that "the loss of a loved animal can have severe negative influences both upon health and emotional states." Moreover, "Psychotic depression and suicide can follow the death of a pet, as well as the less obvious phenomenon of 'giving up' or the 'helplessness-homelessness syndrome' which is frequently a precursor to physical disease."

Dr. Harry Roswell and A. A. McWilliam of the Canadian Council on Animal Care point out, "The death of a pet differs from that of a member of the family, in that in the latter instance the bereaved have the support of relatives and the comfort of their religion. . . . [Either] seems of little solace when a pet dies."

"Many," as Dr. Katcher says, "conceal their grief for fear of frank ridicule."

Sometimes it is the same people who anxiously advise one not to stifle one's grief in the instance of a human loss—"Don't bottle it all up! Let yourself cry!"—who look a little askance when the loss involves a pet. Perhaps whatever ridicule now exists will be assuaged as we come to know more about the impact of the human/animal bond on all our lives.

At the time I married Allen and moved to New York to live, I left Mom and Dad and the three dogs flourishing in California. Within the next six months, my dad had died suddenly of a heart attack, and all three dogs had gone in close succession. My mother went from a full house to nothing in almost no time . . . and I have always been proud of the way she handled her desolation. To speak of losing a husband and the dogs in the same breath may shock some . . . but only Horace White would quite appreciate what it meant to lose the comfort of "the boys" at the time she needed them most. Eventually, she found room in her heart for a new little dog-friend who busied himself making a new place of his own.

In some cases, people need a little push before making that first move. One such incident involved the mother of beautiful Natalie Wood, whose untimely, tragic death left an aching void in all who knew her. Her mother was having a particularly difficult time, understandably. Tranquilizers, social activities, nothing seemed to help. Her doctor, aware that Mrs. Gurdin's little dog had died before Natalie's accident, finally said to her, "You really should get another dog. You'd be surprised how much it would help." By now ready to try anything, Mrs. Gurdin considered several small breeds, finally settling on a poodle—Natalie had always had poodles—and the medicine worked wonders. Instead of taking tranquilizers, Mrs. Gurdin is now actively involved with a charity, the Motion Picture Mothers, and is back in the mainstream. This is not to say that one small poodle was totally responsible for the turnaround, but he certainly helped.

The death of a pet, however tragic, is something every pet owner knows up front he must face sooner or later. We, as humans, have no control over the situation. An equally heartbreaking situation that we *can* influence, however, is the evicting and barring from residence of elderly people who desire animal companionship.

Many elderly people find themselves in need of new housing. . . . Some are on fixed incomes and cannot afford the old family place; others simply cannot manage the old homestead any longer and would like a small efficiency apartment. There are a myriad of other reasons. . . . Such moves in and of themselves can be traumatic. Irene Burnside calls the resulting disorientation "relocation shock." As with children moving to a new neighborhood, the aged often feel less threatened when a loved animal comes along to share in the change.

Unfortunately, the old family pet is not always welcome in the new surroundings. More and more I read of people who have lived with animals all their lives, but who now (after retirement) are faced with moving into smaller, lower-cost, or even government-subsidized housing—with a no-pets policy. The following letter illustrates the frustration:

> I just moved to a low-cost apartment, which I desperately needed. . . . I had to give up my little Doxie, Pepper. . . . I loved her dearly, but had to give her up, which really saddened me. I am alone now, and very lonely without her. All I do now is sit and smoke cigarettes and watch the boob tube. I am only 63, and partially disabled, but my dog helped me to get the exercise I needed. Now I don't care if I ever get out of my chair or not. No one needs me; my dog did.

Janet Nussman, of the Massachusetts Administration on Aging, and Marianna Burt, director of ethical studies, Massachusetts Society for the Prevention of Cruelty to Animals, write of a sixty-one-year-old paralyzed man (a stroke victim) named Frank who, along with his handicapped wife and their nine-year-old terrier companion, Tammy, was evicted from his apartment when the building was converted to condominiums. Forced to turn to public housing, they discovered the rules did not allow for any pets. Frank's doctor even wrote a letter explaining the crucial role Tammy played in the man's life, but to no avail. The best solution was to find a new home for the dog—not always easy when a nine-year-old animal is involved. As Janet and Marianna point out, "At age nine, he is not really adoptable . . . and they are really just waiting for the inevitable—when they must have him humanely put away. But there is nothing humane about putting Frank through the anguish of being without Tammy."

I know from the mail I receive that these stories are not isolated cases but represent a pattern of deprivation involving surprisingly large numbers of older persons today. The Massachusetts SPCA estimates that in Boston alone, at least one hundred pets are forced from their homes and into shelters *each week* by no-pet leases.

The problem seems to be worldwide. "Society seems to go out of its way to make it difficult for the elderly to have pets, to deprive them of the comfort an animal can bring. . . . This should not happen," says the Montreal-based Canadian Society for the Prevention of Cruelty to Animals. Helping to fight the problem there, the Canadian SPCA has made available to the public various pamphlets explaining the rights of tenants.

Because the majority of rental housing in the United States is privately owned, landlords are free to regulate pets as they see fit. A large number of our elderly must therefore choose between retaining longtime companions and seeking more appropriate housing for themselves.

"Since a treasured pet could help ease the inevitable transitions faced by older people," say Janet Nussman and Marianna Burt, "the destruction of that relationship can be devastating."

"Worse, in some large cities when landlords want to free an apartment from rent control, tenants may be evicted under 'no pet' clauses even though they have maintained a pet there for some time *with* the landlord's knowledge."

While we certainly are not seeking to alter the rights of individuals or the free-enterprise system, we do feel that there is room for compromise and compassion where pets for the elderly are concerned.

Public housing is, of course, a much more involved issue, complicated by the fact that there are different *types* of public housing. Housing *subsidized* by federal Housing and Urban Development funds, for example, is still private housing and subject to the whims of individual landlords.

HUD remains silent on the pet issue, allowing local agencies to monitor such decisions.

Government-operated housing, however, is potentially controllable. California, I am happy to say, has recently passed the first state law in the Union protecting the rights of elderly pet owners in housing owned and operated by *any* city, state, or federal agency. Similar laws are in various stages of readiness in legislatures around the country, and change may be on the way.

Janet and Marianna sum up the situation by saying, "For many elderly, a pet is a member of the family (perhaps the only one left), provides a reason for living and caring, and contributes hours of entertainment, affection, and companionship. *It should not be beyond our interest or ability to find ways to facilitate and support this rich relationship* [italics added]."

All the theorizing in the world about what animals mean to certain groups of people cannot describe it nearly as well as looking around at individual pet/person situations one may know.

Madeline Hicks of Carmel, California (Midge to everyone but the bank) and her miniature schnauzer, Toby, are a walking example of the consummate human/animal bond . . . two individuals on the same wave length. Midge is one of the stars of the First Theatre of Monterey (the country's oldest) and is still performing as she celebrates her ninetieth year. Almost totally deaf, and just this side of legally blind, Midge keeps those details to herself, and only her closest friends realize how remarkably she copes. Toby is a bustling little dog, full of himself, and very much the man of the little cottage he shares with his mistress. When he comes visiting with her, he is into everything full tilt, but can always hear Midge's soft-spoken, "Toby," and responds immediately. Many times, when the conversation becomes noisy and general, Midge keeps smiling and participating, but I see her hand creep out to touch Toby, and he snuggles in. She says she can feel the "tone" of the conversation through him. To someone watching, they become a wonderful little island of mutual security.

It isn't always possible to prescribe a relationship like that of Midge and Toby, but sometimes it works well. A doctor, discouraged about his elderly patient in a nursing home, determined to try a different approach. He carefully wrote out a prescription: "one dog." The nursing home modified the man's room, and even better, they took time to find *the appropriate dog*. They evidently did a very good job, as the medication, one dog named Boof, worked wonders.

Sometimes, senior citizens, reluctant to give up their privilege of living alone, will let their own well-being suffer in the interest of independence. Animal owners, however, are less likely to do this. In Scotland, there were cases of elderly people being negligent about keeping their homes warm in wintertime . . . risking serious illness and even death from the loss of body heat. In one group, caged birds were given to them to care for, and they were told the birds would die if the temperature dropped below 65 degrees. The problem was solved. In worrying about the welfare of the animals, these people inadvertently wound up taking care of themselves.

There are times when the family veterinarian may have a better insight into a specific problem than anyone else, especially if he has had a long association with the client. One veterinarian reports that an elderly woman brought in her elderly dog, saying she was worried about his heart problem. (The woman also had heart problems, and both she and the dog were old, both were fat, and both had trouble moving about.) It seems the family who had looked after her had moved away, her apartment was not properly heated, and the woman was patently afraid she couldn't manage on her own. She was unable to admit the dilemma of her own need—even to her physician—but she could convey it through fears that her pet might suffer. In this case, alerted, a social worker arranged for supportive services and had the heat turned up. The woman reported to her vet that her dog's heart trouble had vanished!

While 95 percent of America's elderly live in private residences, the remaining 5 percent live in nursing homes, convalescent homes, and "retirement" homes for the aged. Pets are no less valuable to these people and, in fact, are showing up more and more frequently in such facilities around the country. Dr. Levinson helped lay the groundwork for pet-facilitated therapy in these institutions less than fifteen years ago, when such programs were still considered "shocking."

Dr. Bustad speaks of institutionalizing as "warehousing" our elderly people. He says he first became interested in the influence of pets in nursing-home situations when he took his little dog to visit his mother-in-law. No one at the facility liked the idea—they were afraid someone might trip—so he carried the dog . . . and he still wasn't too popular. Except with the residents themselves who reached out immediately to touch this little bundle of life.

A similar incident involved a member of the board of a large hospital group. An impeccable dresser, the man would tuck his small dog under his well-cut jacket (shades of Bandy!) and sneak him in to visit the man's eighty-five-year-old mother. According to him, his mother was not all that thrilled at seeing her son, but she was really excited about seeing the dog.

Nursing homes have always represented something of a mixed blessing. For some of the residents, arriving at the home stirs an awakening of interests. They are no longer alone and have new neighbors, new friends with whom to share their lives. Living so close to other "soul mates" offers a certain degree of security, particularly to people who feel on the frail side and who used to worry about their safety while living alone.

On the other hand, nursing homes represent desertion for many people, a time when family and friends have died, moved away, or otherwise left them "stranded."

Candace N. Corson, while attending Yale University in 1976, made weekly visits for nearly a year to a convalescent hospital in New Haven. While many topics were discussed with the patients, she reported that five basic themes kept recurring:

• The good effects that it seemed likely would result from care out in the community, in the person's home, if such care could be made feasible.

• Feelings of betrayal by the community, especially by the family, and wishes to have a response from the family.

• Wishes to leave the convalescent hospital, to escape. (These feelings seem to be tied partly to physical ills, such as inability to be up and active, and partly to the real social inability to leave.)

• Thoughts of death, which are, of course, an important problem for the aged of any society to face.

• Methods of handling the situation, ways of "making the most of it" (in the words of one patient), perhaps to make oneself liked and better treated by staff and visitors.

Traditionally, nursing facilities have offered a broad scope of leisure-time activities, everything from fingerpainting to movies to shuffleboard games to Saturday-night dancing. Such organized activities, however, often go unattended by residents who may feel apprehensive about learning new skills, new endeavors. Many elderly people actually fear the failures that accompany new activities. Most important, as Dr. Levinson believes, none of these time fillers actually addresses the basic dilemma of the aging.

The elderly, like the rest of us, have a tremendous need for affection, for companionship, and for the opportunity "to do" for others. Age does not curb these needs and, if anything, makes them stronger. Afternoon games of shuffleboard do little to satisfy them. Pets, however, offer a great deal.

An obedient dog or cat, for instance, can do wonders to restore a nursing-home resident's sense of identity, self-respect, and ego mastery. According to Dr. Levinson, "The trust and confidence a pet demonstrates to his master is sometimes the sole experience of faith in building a bridge to the future. For some of the aged residents of nursing homes, a pet may very well be the only remaining link with reality."

During the fifteen years since Dr. Levinson's theories became topics of public conversation, many nursing facilities have adopted pets as live-in mascots. Others, realizing that even among the aged there are those who do not wish to be around animals, have started "pet visitations"; various local groups bring dogs and cats and other animals into the nursing homes for periodic visits.

The Marin (California) Humane Society, for example, makes weekly visits to the residents of local convalescent centers for the elderly. Puppies, kittens, and lap dogs are favorites among the senior residents, who, as volunteer Kathy Sullivan says, "often identify the animals with a pet they once owned. It's not uncommon for volunteers to witness a flood of emotions when they present a pet to an elderly person."

Charma Clift Rasmussen, director of volunteers for a group called P.A.T. (the Patient Advocacy Team) in Greeley, Colorado, concurs. Her group's "Puppy Program" has been in existence for five years. She told us recently, "Our volunteers take one or two puppies into a nursing home each week and spend the afternoon. They go from room to room and ask each resident if he or she would like to have a little puppy visit them. We have found that very few residents dislike dogs. They may appear apprehensive or withdrawn at first, but as soon as they pat or touch, hold or hug a loving little puppy, memories come flooding back, and very soon the resident will be talking about pets they have owned in the past. (I personally believe that elderly women can associate holding a puppy with holding a baby—something she probably hasn't been able to do for many years.) We make it a point to visit as many room-bound residents as possible, since they are not able to participate in many of the other activities. On a weekly basis, the puppies and volunteers may see twenty to twenty-five people."

The Ottawa (Canada) Humane Society's Pet Visitation Program is currently serving nine area nursing homes and uses a "group encounter" activity similar to that used in many nursing homes here in the States: The residents are seated in a circle, when possible, with the center of the floor covered with newspapers. The residents pet and play with the animals for thirty or forty minutes, and then the animals are placed in the center of the circle, and everyone watches their playful antics. Occasionally, animals are carried to bedridden patients so they may share in the enjoyment.

The Humane Society for Larimer County (Colorado) has been visiting area nursing homes for the past three years, often visiting fifteen to twenty facilities a month. "Several of the facilities have begun to plan other activities around our visits," says education director Cindy Bean. "Two local homes are making catnip toys for us each month, and several other facilities are planning a major

bake sale for our shelter. This is especially encouraging for
the program, knowing that our visits mean so much to so
many people, and being able to promote further response
and activities in the residents beyond our visits!"

At Beverly Manor Convalescent Home in Carmel,
California, I accompanied the Monterey SPCA on one of
its regular visits with a puppy and a cat. It was lovely to see
the warm reception given the pets in general, and the different ways of communicating individually. Some pictures
were taken and the photographer, Flossie Stowell, had an
interesting observation: "Looking through the lens, it
doesn't happen until they *touch!*"

Some facilities of this kind find it is better to have the
same animals brought back each week (perhaps using private pets), so an ongoing relationship can be built up. Others feel the variety of pets and the looking forward to
seeing something different is beneficial.

Dr. Michael McCulloch went one step beyond the obvious reasons why animals in institutional settings can be a
blessing, by suggesting that pets may also have an *indirect*
effect on patients. "Pets may augment staff members' interest and morale, thus increasing their level of verbal and
physical interaction with patients."

Pets, indeed, offer nursing-home residents a great deal
more than fun and diversion. Mathilde Kearny writes of a
program started in Boston in 1976, in which well-behaved
dogs and cats from the Massachusetts SPCA shelters are
offered to eligible nursing homes for adoption. Bonnie, a
three-year-old West Highland terrier, was the first such animal to find a home—and immediately started to "work"
for her room and board. Says Mathilde:

> One rest home resident, addicted to alcohol and
> denied the chance of a home and family, spends

her time following Bonnie around the building, calling her endearing names and seeing that she wants for nothing. From her Bonnie receives the love and attention that might in other, happier circumstances, have been lavished on a child. . . . For another lady, daily walks with Bonnie are a link to the outside world. There is little time to stare out the window fretting about a broken marriage and a family's neglect. . . . To a middle-aged retarded woman, Bonnie gives unreserved love and friendship; their relationship is not hindered by the woman's achievement levels or affected by her physical appearance.

Dr. Bustad tells the story of Handsome, a Persian cat, and the effect he had on Marie, a nursing-home resident. This particular institution established what it referred to as a private therapy room, in which a single patient would live with Handsome. Marie was chosen because, as Dr. Bustad says, "she had no family or friends, would not communicate, and remained curled in the fetal position with no interest in living. She also had sores on her legs from continual scratching."

Once they were established as roommates, Handsome changed things: Whenever Marie tried to scratch her legs, Handsome would play with her hands or otherwise distract her. He gave her something to do. Within a month the sores were healed. Marie became fascinated by the cat and started asking the staff about his care. Before long, she was even inviting other residents in to visit with her roomie.

"Now," Dr. Bustad reports, "she converses with strangers, as well as the nursing home staff, about the cat and other subjects."

In 1975, Roger Mugford and J. G. M'Comisky conducted a study in England of groups of seventy-five- to eighty-one-year-olds. The purpose was "to determine the feasibility of field experimentation into the effects of pets upon the social attitudes and mental and physical health" of pet owners. The pensioners were divided into a control group and two experimental groups. One of the latter groups was given begonia plants to care for, and the other was given budgerigars (Australian parakeets). At the end of the study, Mugford and M'Comisky discovered that the group receiving the birds showed improvement in their attitudes toward people and toward their own psychological health. They said:

> Our overwhelming impression from the study is that the old people in our budgerigar groups had formed a surprisingly intimate (and presumably rewarding) attachment to these unsolicited pet birds. We found on our visits that they had become such a powerful topic of conversation that they could even displace the monotonous awareness and discussions of past and pending medical ailments.

Drs. Samuel and Elizabeth Corson, who in 1975 introduced pets into a psychiatric hospital ward at Ohio State University, in 1976 relocated their research team to the Castle Nursing Home in Millersburg, Ohio. At first, staff people at the home were against bringing pets onto the premises, but Dr. Sam persuaded the home's administrators that the pet-therapy project "might help elderly residents and simplify work for the staff."

In a speech presented in Stockholm in June of that year, the Corsons summarized their findings:

> Old people often relate positively to the pet in non-verbal communication and tactile interac-

tions. Then gradually the circle of social interaction widens to include at first the therapist who
introduced the pet, and later other patients and
nursing-home personnel. The initial non-verbal
forms of interaction may eventually be enriched
and strengthened with verbal communication and
wholesome emotional expressions and warmth.

The Corsons told of two very contrary elderly ladies,
Verna and Madge, who were roommates at the nursing
home. These two fought with the staff and as often as not
with each other. A wirehaired fox terrier was introduced to
them, and the ladies calmed down admirably. The Corsons
state,

> A series of interactions ensued, involving competi-
> tion, rejection, curiosity, and interest. Sometimes
> both ladies would pet the dog; at other times, one
> of the ladies would reject the dog while the room-
> mate petted the animal. Some of the other resi-
> dents showed a distinct interest in the transactions
> and enjoyed the session very much. The nursing
> staff believes that although the pet did not cause
> any detectable personality changes at the individ-
> ual level, the dog was the agent in creating im-
> proved social interactions *between* the two ladies.
> After Verna and Madge had a few sessions of pet-
> facilitated psychotherapy, together with Fluff,
> they became more tolerant of each other.

As far back as 1975, the Divine Savior Nursing Home
in Portage, Wisconsin, added a young canine therapist
named Princess to its staff. Sister Regina, administrator of
the home, told *Shoptalk* magazine that the change in morale that Princess effected was almost instantaneous. "Resi-

dents who hadn't responded much to anything are petting Princess and grinning from ear to ear."

"Pet therapy works in an institutional situation because it's a very stereotyped situation, with no room for novelty, individuality, or privacy," says Dr. Michael McCulloch. "Animals give a sense of time and help to orient people."

The thirty-two women living at San Francisco's Episcopal Retirement Home for Ladies have adopted two live-in felines, Susy and Sally, who, as one resident puts it, "give us something to talk about, complain about, argue about, and reminisce about. . . . We love them."

Sometimes, of course, animals—particularly cats—have been known to adopt people. A stray cat named Ginger, for example, wandered onto the grounds of Paradise Villa Nursing Home in Moscow, Idaho, and took up permanent residence. Elderly residents began leaving food and milk for her, and in a matter of days the home's administrators noticed a new vitality in the air.

Rita McMillan, activities director at Paradise Villa, indicates that while not all the residents like having the cat around, those who do often had such pets as children. The animal makes the facility "more like a home." The residents "don't feel they're losing part of their life because they've come to a nursing home."

Dr. Leo Bustad, whose offices at Washington State University are only eight miles from Paradise Villa, remarks, "In nursing homes, animals give residents something to think about instead of their own physical complaints. . . . Physical defects or personal appearance have never affected an animal's friendship."

The doctor is the first to caution, however, that merely placing an animal—just any animal—with the elderly is not enough, and indiscriminate placements can do more harm than good. Nursing homes must make sure that the pet-therapy programs have a high probability for success. "In too many situations," the doctor says, "animals have been placed with people or in institutions without studying the circumstances, instructing the recipients in care and therapy procedures, and providing follow-up visits to evaluate the effectiveness of the animal."

He cites a case in point in which the activity director of a nursing home decided it would be nice for the residents to have a small caged gerbil for company. The idea was a disaster—several of the residents beat on the cage and tried to kill the animal. Why? Many of the residents, the director learned later, had farming backgrounds, and looked upon gerbils with the same disdain they'd always had for rats. Obviously, this activity director's heart was in the right place, but his head did not think the idea through. It is very critical that the *proper animal* be selected for *each* pet-therapy situation.

Jean Grover, a member of the Humane Society of Wright County (Minnesota), warns of a few other easily remedied problem areas that one must watch out for: Visiting children are often sent off by visiting parents to "go play with the animals so we grown-ups can talk." Often the children have absolutely no knowledge of how to care for the pets, and trouble ensues. This habit should not be allowed.

Many residents try to "win favors" with pets by giving them food and between-meal treats, which have been found to create health and overweight problems for the animals. Bribery is a bummer.

Many residents will not allow an animal to be caged or restricted to a given area, claiming "it's cruel." However, a little diplomatic explanation can usually clarify the situation. Everyone must be made aware of the rules and regulations up front, to protect the safety of both the residents *and* the pets.

Some people, of course, have a built-in concern about whether animals in nursing facilities will bring in germs and cause illness among the residents. Dorothy Walster, of the Scottish Health Education Unit, in replying to such doubts, asserts that standards of hygiene must, of course, be maintained so that no patient or pet is allowed to suffer. However, "there is no reason why diseases should be transmitted to the elderly by their pets any more than to any other age groups, and prejudices should be removed by public education."

Albert Kushlick makes an interesting distinction between the types of agents affecting the elderly. He speaks of doctors, social workers, psychologists, administrators, and others, as "hit and run" people, as distinguished from those who are with them around the clock—the "continuing care" people—family members, nurses, etc. Pets, far from being "hit and run," certainly fall into the "continuing care" category.

Pets, however, for one reason or another, are not permitted in all nursing-home facilities; indeed, many communities have laws on the books making such animals illegal.

But some change for the better may be in the wind. The state of Minnesota passed a law in 1979, permitting nursing homes to keep pets on the premises, "subject to reasonable rules as to the care, type, and maintenance of the pet." Fair enough!

In 1981, the First International Conference on the Human/Animal Bond, Philadelphia, drafted and approved a resolution that was submitted to the White House, calling for an end to the cruelty of separating the aged from their pets, and "to establish humane policies and regulations insuring that the human/companion animal bond can remain intact for responsible pet owners" regardless of age.

Dr. Bustad, himself raised on a farm, feels that one

terrible thing we do to older people—those who have a feeling for animals—is to remove them to a convalescent, nursing, or retirement home, or an apartment where pets are not allowed.

"One of the big rewards of having loved animals all your life," he says, "is the fact that you could be spared a lonely old age as a result of your continuing affection. . . . There are two times when you need animals the most . . . when you are very young, and when you are very old . . . and often quite a bit in between."

Part Two

Just What the Doctor Ordered

"To know there is an eye will mark your coming and look brighter when you come . . ."

—LORD BYRON

5.

A Level Called Interdependence

In Norway, in 1966, a blind musician named Erling Stordahl established Beitostolin, a rehabilitation center for the handicapped with a sports orientation. Horses and dogs play an active part in the heavy emphasis on physical therapy. Blind persons are taught not only to ride horses, but to ski.

The idea of a blind skier would seem incredible to me had I never known my dear friend Tom Sullivan. You know Tom as a singer, songwriter, actor, author. His autobiography, *If You Could See What I Hear,* was made into a movie and gives some idea of this remarkable young man's accomplishments.

Blind since birth, or "inconvenienced" as Tom puts it, he grew up using his lack of sight as a goad to conquer the things most of his sighted friends find too difficult. He not only skis, he surfs, golfs, is a long-distance runner, has driven a motorcycle, and has made thirty-seven sky dives. He is proudest of being beautiful Patty's beloved husband, and the father of two great kids, Blythe and Tommy. Not wanting to get rusty, Tom is joining Blythe in the jumping class at the Santa Barbara Horse Show.

Tom's lovely golden retriever guide dog, Dinah, is his constant companion. She has her work cut out for her . . .

perhaps even more than most, since she accompanies him on his many trips around the country for concerts and speaking engagements. Dinah is all business when she is in harness, and watching her work is one of life's better experiences. When she's out of her "girdle," however, she is a relaxed homebody sharing the family with Buster, a German shepherd, and Season, a tiny Maltese. Patty says Dinah isn't above competing for Tom's undivided attention, making no secret of her joy on the occasions when Patty decides not to go along on one of the trips. According to Patty, Dinah merely tolerates her as "your wife," but her hands on Dinah as she says it let you know that theirs is a very special relationship as well.

It is the blind, of course, who gave the public its first awareness of how useful animals can be with the handicapped. Far newer to our society than dogs for the blind are dogs to assist the deaf—hearing-ear dogs. But not all physically handicapped persons are either deaf or blind; there are many cruel, crippling diseases that render people unable to fully take care of themselves. Now, in the wake of human/animal bond research, dogs are trained to help these people. (There have even been some efforts to train monkeys as extra hands for paraplegics, but the jury is still out on the long-range success of these experiments.) We will explore each of these fields, but first, where did it all begin . . . and where is it going?

The earliest known use of animals with the handicapped was at York Retreat in England. Established in 1792 by the Society of Friends, it was started as a "Christian and common sense" alternative to the rather barbaric lunatic asylums of the day. Punishment and restraints were not used here and every effort was made to have the patient lead as normal a life as possible . . . even being encouraged to dress in his own clothes. Gardens were pop-

ulated with small animals—rabbits and poultry—in the
hope that patients would learn self-control by caring for
something that needed their help. According to Dr. Michael McCulloch, "This non-punitive treatment system,
emphasizing acceptance and natural surroundings of a 'living environment,' formed the basis of humane treatment
standards that are still applicable today."

Some seventy-five years after York was established, a
treatment center for the physically and mentally handicapped was founded in Germany. A group of Christians in
Westphalia purchased a place which they called Bethel,
meaning "House of God," and the first residents were epi-
leptics. Friedrich and Fritz von Bodelschwingh, father and
son, were the institution's first directors. Both farm animals
and household pets were an integral part of Bethel's treatment center from the very beginning; later, actual farms
were developed so that all the residents who could work or
do something useful had the opportunity to participate.

It was Fritz who saved Bethel from its greatest threat,
that of Nazi Germany. Dr. Leo K. Bustad, Washington
State University, writing in *The Latham Letter,* tells the
story:

> Hitler put out the order that all people who were
> considered disabled would be put to death. This
> would include, of course, all the patients at
> Bethel. Fritz refused to fill out the forms that were
> required, but officials came and completed them
> for all the patients. Fritz appealed to the high
> command, but received unsatisfactory answers.
>
> One day, officials came from Berlin to make
> final arrangements. Hitler's personal physician
> apparently was one of these. Fritz got him off to
> the side and asked him what really determined
> whether a person is 'less than human.' The answer

he got was that the criterion was the individual's ability to communicate. Fritz asked the doctor to accompany him to see Bethel's most handicapped residents in House Patmos. He reviewed various cases of children and adults, and demonstrated that communication did take place. On completing the rounds, Fritz turned to his visitor from Berlin and said, 'Although *you* may not be able to communicate with every one of these people, it should be obvious to you that *we* do.'

On returning to headquarters, Hitler's physician said to his associate, 'We have ceased negotiations at Bethel.' Not one of the patients at Bethel was a victim of this cruel oppression. During the war, provisions were somehow made for all of them through free-will offerings. They were saved because people with great compassion took time to listen to those who were hard to listen to.

Today the animal therapy programs have been expanded to include not only farm animals and personal pets, but a wild animal game park, rather elaborate bird aviaries, and an indoor stadium for horseback riding.

Perhaps the most encouraging thing about Bethel has always been its point of view. As Dr. Bustad reports, "Every attempt is made not to say, 'This person is handicapped,' and 'This is a staff member!' Visitors are often surprised as to who are the patients and who are the staff."

It wasn't until 1942 that formal use of animals for therapy was initiated here in the United States, when they were introduced at the Army Air Force Convalescent Hospital at Pawling, New York. Veterans convalescing from battle injuries or emotional trauma were encouraged to work with livestock—cattle, horses, and poultry. The hospital grounds also included an extensive parkland, where the veterans could encounter wild animals, once again to channel their attention away from themselves and toward constructive therapy. Unfortunately, no quantitative information was recorded as to the effects of the animals on the men.

This last seems to be a chronic problem, and points up a great frustration shared by everyone involved with pet-assisted therapy: the lack of recorded results kept through the years. Time and time again accounts of tremendously productive activities end with "few records were kept" or "few comparative testing results available." This unfortunate lack has inhibited the acceptance of the whole idea by some segments of the medical community—those who, of necessity, need facts and figures to support anecdotal information.

Because virtually all the programs using animal-facilitated therapy consist of small groups scattered over the world, working to the limit of their funds and therefore understaffed, few really know *how* to document their findings. Thankfully, times are changing.

The enormous need to distill the countless case histories down into usable comparative statistics is being met head on at Washington State University. Dr. Bustad, whom we have quoted previously, is dean of the College of Veterinary Medicine and founder of the People-Pet Partnership Program. Dr. Bustad has set up a computerized data bank where the input from all the individual cases can be sorted and evaluated. Not until we stepped into the computer age has such an assessment been attainable, and it could be that, finally, we are at the right place at the right time.

To evaluate the benefits derived from the therapeutic use of pets, as well as the potential problems inherent in the programs, more information is needed as to what constitutes the relationship between man and animal under *normal* circumstances. Easier said than done when one considers the variety of animals and the innumerable human situations involved.

Dr. Michael McCulloch says that we are in the position of having to subject various pet-therapy programs to rigorous scientific testing, when the belief is that these programs already work. He adds, "If pet therapy offers relief from human suffering, then it is our professional obligation to explore every available avenue for its use."

One pet-therapy program that has withstood the test of time is the use of dogs as guides for the blind. The sight of a dog wearing the traditional square harness is familiar to us all, and never fails to elicit an appreciative smile from passersby. But it was not always so, particularly in this country.

The idea of using specially trained dogs to lead the blind originated in Germany during World War I. Prior to this, blind individuals were totally dependent on other people for assistance in mobility. The war, however, resulted in great numbers of blind German veterans being discharged into war-torn communities where human help was simply not available.

The Germans had been very successful in training dogs for various types of military duty, so it seemed a logical next step to work out a program in which the animals could help the blinded veterans. This was in 1916, when a program was started at Oldenburg using German shepherds; the dogs learned quickly and more schools were added.

Because of the postwar anti-German sympathies, or skepticism perhaps, the use of guide dogs did not spread far.

One American woman, however, did ultimately prove instrumental in bringing the German ideas to the United States. In 1923 Dorothy Harrison Eustis, her husband,

George, and her German shepherd, Hans, founded the Fortunate Fields research, breeding, and training center for German shepherds in Vevey, Switzerland. Four years later, Mrs. Eustis contributed an article to *The Saturday Evening Post,* telling about the dogs being trained in various German schools to help the blind. When a Tennessee lad named Morris Frank, himself blind, heard about the article, he wrote to Mrs. Eustis seeking her help in acquiring such a dog. He ultimately traveled to Switzerland, where a Fortunate Fields dog was trained especially for him. Frank returned to the United States, and in 1929, through sheer persistence, helped Mrs. Eustis establish the Seeing Eye guide-dog school in Morristown, New Jersey. For many years this would be the *only* organized nonprofit school devoted to the training and placement of guide dogs in all of North America.

By the late thirties, threats of war were again sweeping through Europe, and many Germans—including many guide-dog specialists—emigrated to the United States.

In 1938, Leader Dogs for the Blind was established in Detroit, and cooperation was immediately established with The Seeing Eye. The purpose was far too important for petty rivalries. The new school placed eighteen dogs with blind masters in its first year.

World War II finally erupted and like Germany twenty-five years earlier, the United States shuddered as more and more of its veterans returned home blinded by battle but not willing to become dependent on society. The initial success of The Seeing Eye and Leader Dogs for the Blind, combined with the immense popularity of two magnificent German shepherd movie stars, Strongheart and Rin Tin Tin, proved to Americans that dogs could indeed be trained in almost unbelievable skills.

Through the years, many new guide-dog enterprises were started, until at one time there were almost thirty of them around the country. Those that were mismanaged or put together too hastily soon folded. Today there are nine, foremost among which are still The Seeing Eye, Leader Dogs, and Guide Dogs for the Blind in San Rafael, California. One school in Los Angeles, International Guiding Eyes, uses only spayed females in their program, calling them their "leading ladies."

Guide Dogs for the Blind, begun in 1942, is located about twenty miles north of San Francisco, and can accommodate up to twenty-four students at a time.

Only three breeds of dogs are used—the German shepherd, the golden retriever, and the Labrador retriever. Other schools have been known to include yet additional breeds in their programs, but Guide Dogs have found these three to be the most satisfactory for their purposes. All three breeds have coats that are adaptable to hot and cold climates, are easy to groom, are of medium size, have calm temperaments, and are willing workers. The school maintains its own breeding stock, and only in occasional, exceptional cases is a donated dog accepted from the outside.

When the puppies born at the school kennels reach six weeks of age, they begin a five-week testing period by a corps of volunteers, who check their reactions to strange sounds and obstacles, as well as their overall intelligence.

At eleven weeks these puppies are adopted by young 4-H members throughout the western states, for a period of one year to fifteen months, for experience in a family atmosphere. If the adult dog is to be a stable, sound companion later on, the affection and people-orientation he receives in this socialization period is vital. There are five to six hundred of these "farm outs" currently being raised throughout the West, and the requirements are a fenced yard, a good diet, and nearly twenty-four-hour human companionship.

The little ones, of course, need love and the usual assortment of family experiences, but the commitment goes a
little beyond that with the average family pet. As well as
learning simple obedience and going along on family outings, these puppies accompany their humans to the grocery
store, walk in traffic, and ride on public transportation. To
preclude any complaints, these little workers wear green
jackets that identify them as Guide Dog puppies. Or prep-
pies, as it were. This period of family orientation lasts until
the dogs are anywhere from fifteen to eighteen months of
age. At this point the young people bring their charges
back to the school to begin the formal guide-dog training.
The dogs don't all make it. Some are disqualified at this
juncture if there is any evidence of a physical ailment, or if
they exhibit any inability to learn obedience—but there is
no stigma attached. If the dog is dropped, for any reason,
the 4-H family that raised him has the option of taking him
back. (The school has a waiting list of one to two years of
families who want to adopt the so-called rejects.)

Several years ago Allen produced and I wrote and
hosted a television show called *The Pet Set.* On one program
we devoted the entire half hour to animals helping the
blind. I interviewed a group of these 4-H youngsters, and
asked how difficult it was for them to have to give up a
puppy after all those months of close association. Each of
them said that having gone into the project *knowing* it was
a temporary arrangement, plus the pride of accomplishment, helped a great deal. Sure, it hurt at the moment of
parting, but the thrill of coming back later to watch their
"baby" graduate made up for it all. Many of these young
people turn right around and take on a new charge to raise.

Once training begins, each licensed instructor is responsible for a string of twelve to fifteen dogs, which he
trains for four to five months. The first step, of course, is to
teach the dogs the basic obedience commands, such as

"come," "sit," "down," "fetch." Each dog must also learn to work in harness and master the commands "forward," "left," and "right." It will take a dog five or six workouts before he is ready to advance to the residential area of San Rafael. Here the instructor teaches the dog to stop for up and down curbs, and to make left and right turns, encouraging him with lots of praise each time the dog shows a willingness to please.

By now the dog should be ready to move to a new section of San Rafael, with more pedestrians and heavy traffic. Here he learns to cross a street in a straight line, work around obstructions, pay attention to moving traffic, etc. The dog will then begin working in stores, buildings, elevators, and stairways. The next step is training in San Francisco, where he will be worked in a downtown area. Here, in very heavy traffic, the dog must show initiative and responsibility in order to get around safely.

(There is a Guide Dog training film that I shall never forget, showing a Labrador retriever—born and bred through generations to be a bird dog—leading his instructor through a huge flock of pigeons on the city street. As the cloud of birds exploded around him, the dog continued his steady pace, glancing neither right nor left.)

The instructor, now blindfolded, will then work the dog, and if the team passes the test, the dog is ready for his new blind master, who, in many cases, has been waiting for over a year.

This school, like many others, is supported solely by contributions from the general public. Although the cost of training the dog and master comes to about $6,000, the dogs are provided to the blind free of charge.

A guide dog can be a bridge between the sighted and blind worlds and can help people lead productive lives. One Guide Dog for the Blind graduate, Pinky Dukes, of

Seaside, California, is an instructor at the Adaptive Center at Monterey Peninsula College. He speaks of his guide dog, Ivan: "Having Ivan has changed my life. I gained mobility and independence. I don't have to grab somebody's arm to do things. I've started to depend on myself. Having Ivan enables me to take the bus. I stop every day at the market and then walk nine blocks home."

The human/companion animal bond works in both directions. I once heard a story that has always stayed in my mind: A young girl registered into a large hotel with her guide dog in harness, was greeted by the manager, and shown to her room. Much later that night, the manager happened to see her leaving the room, sans dog, and quite obviously sighted. He confronted her, demanding an explanation. Tearfully, she explained, "I had no choice. I know you don't permit dogs in your hotel, and I couldn't leave him. You see, *he's* the one who's blind!"

Another concept, that of hearing dogs for the deaf, apparently dates back only as far as 1968, when a Denver family sought assistance in training the family dog to help their deaf daughter with the sounds heard around the house.

The first actual hearing-dog program was started in 1975 as a "pilot study" under the jurisdiction of Agnes McGrath of the Minnesota Society for the Prevention of Cruelty to Animals. Miss McGrath, a trainer and kennel supervisor, trained a total of six dogs to assist deaf people, and it wasn't long before the center was inundated with requests from deaf people all over the United States. The success of this pilot program led to the Hearing Ear Program of the American Humane Association in 1976.

The field, though certainly still new, is growing every day. There is even a hearing-ear program now on the curriculum at Newbury Junior College in Holliston, Massachusetts, where students at the vocational college can learn to become professional hearing-dog trainers.

Each of the centers currently in operation trains an average of thirty-five to forty dogs a year. This sounds great until one discovers that there are more than fourteen million hearing-impaired people in the United States, at least two million of whom are completely deaf. American Sign Language is the third most common language "spoken" in this country today.

There are many similarities—and a few marked differences—between the procedures of the seeing-eye and the hearing-ear programs. Hearing-ear dogs are trained to do just that—to hear—and to call the sound to the attention of their humans.

It was my privilege to attend a Hearing Ear demonstration at the Los Angeles SPCA. Puffin, a silky little black-and-white mix, and her owner/trainer, Kris Winship, went through the basic steps that would be used in a day-to-day work situation. Though quite small, Puffin was not to be denied when she insisted Kris follow her to a doorbell or a ringing telephone. To differentiate between a smoke alarm and all the other sounds, Puffin would urgently get her mistress's attention, then drop to the floor. This, rather than lead her toward the sound and into possible danger. Watching that busy little body was an education.

All dogs used in the program are six to eighteen months old and are selected from the unwanted animals abandoned at animal shelters. They can be any type of dog and almost any size. Both males and females selected are spayed or neutered before being placed.

Each prospective Hearing Ear dog undergoes a thorough evaluation designed to test the animal's curiosity, temperament, stability, and trainability. Approximately 50 percent of those tested are accepted for training, at which time they proceed to a thorough medical examination to ensure healthy animals for training and placement.

Generally it costs $2,500 to train and place each dog, but the recipients receive the dog free of charge, since the Hearing Ear program is funded solely by donations from concerned citizens. There is no dollar value, however, that can be put on these dogs who fill such a need for self-sufficiency on the part of the recipient. How do you price that out?

The average training time for each dog is three to four months with an instructor, after which training is transferred to the new deaf user.

The actual placement of the dog requires a trainer to deliver a dog personally to the new home. The trainer stays three or four days, until the dog transfers his allegiance to the new owner. After a few months, there is a follow-up visit to smooth out any problems, to be sure the dog is getting the proper care, and to verify that the owner is using the dog to its full potential. As one authority put it, "Too much time and money is spent on these dogs for them to end up as just pets."

"It would be easy to spoil a good dog like Buddy," commented one deaf owner. "If I hadn't kept his training up, they would have taken him back. I wasn't going to let that happen."

Once the probation period is over, the dog is graduated and receives the special-blaze orange collar and leash, as well as a certificate identifying him as an official Hearing Ear dog.

We have mentioned Dr. Leo K. Bustad earlier as one of the prime movers in the human/companion animal bond movement. In the course of conversation about something totally unrelated, Dr. Bustad happened to mention that his wife is hearing-impaired and uses a dog as a hearing aid. And not just any dog. Mrs. Bustad, or "the Chief," as her husband calls her, went through a rigorous, supervised training program *with her own pet,* Bridgette, who had been with them for six years. Dingbat—that's her nickname, not a criticism—responds to all important environmental sounds: doorbells, door knocks, telephone, smoke alarm, alarm clock, teakettle, oven timer. She took to her training readily, eager to please her family. In the case of the smoke alarm, she had to overcome six years of being taught not to jump on the bed and to learn that it was now a requirement in order to alert her mistress. Humans certainly don't make it easy!

In most states a Hearing Ear dog may accompany its master in public buildings and restaurants, on airplanes, buses, etc. He has the same rights as a guide dog, even in the eyes of the Internal Revenue Service. The ruling is that a partially deaf person can deduct, as a medical expense, a dog or cat trained as a hearing aid.

Ralph Dennard is the director of the San Francisco SPCA Hearing Program. Some of his case histories rival any Hollywood scenario:

Pat Holsonbake, an employee of Modesto's Independent Living Council for the Disabled, reports that she owes her life to Bandit, her one-year-old German shepherd. Bandit woke Mrs. Holsonbake one morning during a dangerous gas leak in their home. Pat's cat had apparently turned on the gas while playing in the kitchen, and the deadly fumes were filling the house. Although Bandit had not been trained specifically to detect hazardous smells, he sensed trouble and awakened Pat to the danger.

John and Janet Henry of Pacifica, California, tell of another life-or-death situation involving their hearing dog, Cookie. Both Janet and John have been deaf since birth and have long since learned to cope with their handicap. A complication arose, however, with the birth of their daughter, Elizabeth. John rigged a speaker in Elizabeth's nursery that would flash a light in the Henrys' bedroom whenever she awakened and cried, but John worried about what would happen if he and Janet were asleep. When Cookie arrived on the scene, responding to the baby's cries was one of Cookie's assignments. One night Elizabeth awakened with a heavy chest cold, coughing and struggling to breathe.

"The dog woke us!" John exclaimed proudly. "She jumped on the bed and woke us up! We could tell it was important. Cookie knows the difference between regular cries and cries of panic or pain."

The Henrys dashed to their daughter's room, finding her choking so painfully that her face was turning blue.

"Thank God, she was okay," John says today. "We knew what to do and she was fine after we got there. But without Cookie, what would have happened to our baby?"

Then there was the story about Fifi, a little black spaniel, owned by Vicki Gordon, a San Jose woman. Fifi loves to go on outings and ride in the car. On one drive, she jumped on the back of the seat and started to bark quite diligently at something behind them. Mrs. Gordon checked her rearview mirror and discovered a fire truck approaching with siren blaring and lights flashing. On another occasion, Fifi began to paw and sniff the floorboards, calling Vicki's immediate attention to the fact that they had a tire going flat. My question: At what point does the specific teaching give way to judgment on the part of the dog? It seems next to impossible to train for certain unexpected situations—a flat tire, for instance.

Most of the stories I've heard about pets working with the deaf have involved people like the Henrys and Mrs. Holsonbake and Mrs. Gordon, who have graduated from one hearing-ear school or another. I recently ran across a case history of Theresa Stratthaus, however, whose situation and interaction with her dog, Sharona, is truly unique.

Theresa, it seems, was born "different" and thought to be retarded for many years, until a therapist discovered she suffered from a severe loss of hearing, caused first by a birth defect and later by a spreading infection.

"During those early days," Theresa reflects, "the world was a hateful place, full of searing pain in my inner ears, periods of vertigo, tauntings by other children, and loneliness . . . terrible loneliness. My parents were kind and hardworking and earnest, but they didn't know how to cope with their misfit daughter. And even *I* thought that I was stupid and worthless. Why was I alive, I often wondered."

Once properly diagnosed, Theresa went on to learn lipreading, but ultimately became totally deaf and needed a wheelchair while recovering from vertigo.

Getting back up on crutches after two years, Theresa decided the time was right to adopt a pet. "I wanted a friend," she says.

It was at the North Shore Animal League in Port Washington, New York, that she found Sharona, and Theresa could not believe the sign on her cage. It read, "My name is Sharona. I am deaf, but I know sign language."

"A *deaf* dog! I could hardly believe my eyes! Putting aside my crutches, I sat down and began signing, 'Hello, my name is Theresa. I'm deaf, too. Do you think we could become friends?'"

Well, Sharona had some sign language of her own. Her brown-spotted ears perked up, and her white, short-haired body wiggled all over.

Needless to say, Theresa and Sharona were made for each other, and Theresa soon taught her new pet to come, jump up and down, give a kiss, even—after months of coaxing—to *speak* for a toy bone.

Recalling the incident, Theresa says, "My mouth flew

open, I almost dropped the bone. She was overwhelmed. I was overwhelmed. We hugged. We touched noses. I shouted and cheered, and she barked and rolled over and over, and barked again. She had learned one of the hardest lessons for the deaf . . . *to bring sounds out of a silent world!* This was a major accomplishment for Sharona, and for me. My lonely void was being filled; I was helping another creature. . . ."

So far, cats have not been included in the hearing-ear programs. This is certainly not due to any lack of intelligence on their part, but supposedly because cats are known for their independence and cannot be relied on for assistance quite as consistently as a dog can. However, the Carnation Pet Food Company sponsored a Hero Cat Award each year for ten years; the honoree was chosen from scores of entries relating acts of heroism by cats that benefited the people they loved. On that same *Pet Set* series we mentioned earlier, we featured one of these special felines along with his mistress, Mrs. Elsie Schneider. The cat, Rhubarb, had learned to act as a seeing-eye cat. We shot special film showing the two working together. Not long ago, when Carnation presented its Hero Cat of the Decade Award, it went to none other than our old friend Rhubarb. The award was made posthumously, and accepted by Mrs. Schneider, just one month after Rhubarb had finally gone to rest.

The seeing-eye and hearing-ear successes have set the pattern for another whole new field of assistance for the physically impaired. Dogs are now being trained to serve those people who are in wheelchairs. They serve in a variety of ways over and above the companionship and protection that is built in. They carry packages, retrieve dropped items, turn lights on and off, help with shopping . . . there seems to be no limit to their adaptation to individual situations.

Most of these programs educate the dogs, then put them together with the people in need of assistance for yet an additional training interval of adjustment to living and working together.

Handi-Dogs, Inc., a nonprofit organization in Tucson, Arizona, is unique in that the dog and the person he will be serving train together from the very beginning, forming a bond between them uninterrupted by a third party.

Handi-Dogs and its approach is the brainchild of one Alamo Reaves. Bitsy, as she is known to her many friends, was stricken with rheumatoid arthritis when she was in her freshman year at Columbia University. She found herself constantly dropping things and unable to retrieve them. Having been an animal lover all her life, she wondered if a dog could be trained to help her. On crutches, she tried to take her dog through obedience training, but, in her words, "It was a disaster!" Still she persisted until she had met the challenge. Realizing how much this could mean to others, and with the help of good friends, Handi-Dogs began to grow.

The first small class of nine students and dogs was based strictly on trial and error. Started in 1974, ostensibly as a class to teach dogs basic obedience, it soon became apparent that more than dog training was taking place—the students were experiencing a tremendous psychological boost.

Through the work of dedicated volunteers, today Handi-Dogs offers twelve-week courses to the disabled, the deaf, and senior citizens, whose animals enable them to "enjoy living rather than merely endure life." Founder Bitsy Reaves feels she couldn't have accomplished this had she been nondisabled; as it is, she can empathize with the physical and psychological frustrations that go with this kind of life, because she has been there.

Bitsy was moved to start the program when she found disabled friends longing for the support she received from her own dogs. (She has bred cocker spaniels, and her own Handi-Dog is a mahogany sheltie named Mog.) Bitsy says, "It never occurred to me that a dog-training program could be used to bring isolated people back to the mainstream of life, or to lift depressed people out of despair." She went on to tell me that at least twice in her life her dogs, and her concern for what would happen to them, kept her from committing suicide . . . "and I sure am glad they did!"

"You tend to lose your sense of worthiness and wallow in self-pity. But a dog loves you even when you don't like yourself, and I find it hard to stay depressed very long with my dogs needing me and telling me, in their own way, how wonderful I am."

Handi-Dogs go through the standard beginning obedience training exercises, then go on to more individually designed behavior—picking up dropped objects, barking on command, fetching newspapers, etc. The keynote of the training is to get the owner, in whatever manner possible, to give the dog his commands.

All dogs who go through the program will not be Certified Handi-Dogs. Many are pets of owners who feel it is mutually beneficial to take the course together. It can serve as a pattern for the owner to continue training his animal in areas specifically tailored to his needs at home. It also does a great job of generating self-esteem.

To attain the official status of Certified Handi-Dog, certain procedures are undertaken. Alamo Reaves, or one of her staff, combs the local shelters to find an appropriate dog to suit the individual. They look for a dog who is alert, willing to learn, healthy, and of medium size. After the animal has been put through complete training, it must pass an evaluation test required by state law. A laminated card is presented at graduation, designating that this *Certified Handi-Dog* is entitled to the same privileges as guide dogs and hearing dogs in those states approving.

The city of Tucson regards Handi-Dogs so highly they built them a special training area in a city park with a hardtop work surface, wheelchair facilities, and shade.

A few years ago, an eighty-eight-year-old woman, Lily Passano, put her two terriers, Yin and Yang, through the program successfully. She became so taken with the work of Handi-Dogs that she returned to work as a volunteer and is still there at age ninety-five.

The American Kennel Club has modified its obedience trials so that it is possible for someone in a wheelchair to compete with nondisabled persons on an equal basis. Stewart Nordensson, a cerebral palsy victim with advanced spasticity, took advantage of this opportunity. A member of the Handi-Dog group from the early days, he proceeded to take his yellow Labrador, Beverly, through CD (Companion Dog) and CDX (Companion Dog Excellent) and is now working on her third degree, UD (Utility Dog) . . . all against nonhandicapped competition.

Another group using dogs in this way is Canine Companions for Independence, located in Santa Rosa, California. The same community-training method used so successfully in San Rafael by Guide Dogs for the Blind has been followed by CCI. The Girl Scouts of America, Future Farmers of America, 4-H members, and other children are raising CCI puppies in their homes for one year, at which time the dogs are returned for training. The breeds used in this case are collies, golden retrievers, Labrador retrievers, and Doberman pinschers.

Kerry Klaus, CCI's first participant in 1975, found her life totally changed by her service dog, a Labrador named

Abdul. In the two years they trained together, Kerry learned to be in control of the dog, and Abdul learned to take care of his mistress. Today, he turns lights on and off for her, carries her packages, pushes the call buttons for elevators, picks up things she drops or needs. He also turns on the heater in the van she drives, and accompanies her to her college classes, carrying her books and supplies. He goes shopping with her, picking merchandise off the shelves with his mouth. He even helps her cash a check. Abdul is trained to jump up to the teller's window with Kerry's check in his mouth. He presents it to the teller, who cashes it and puts the money in Abdul's mouth. The teller's face must have been a study the first time this happened.

In all, Abdul knows eighty-five different commands. To quote Kerry, "He is trained to aid me by performing physical tasks that are impossible for me to do on my own. In spite of the fact that I am a full-time college student and hold a part-time job, I spend the bulk of the day requiring no assistance other than that of my faithful companion. The work that he does has enabled me to cut the amount of time I pay hired attendants by two thirds."

Kerry says Abdul also helps in social situations. "He seems to make people immediately at ease with relating to me in spite of the fact they may be acutely uncomfortable about my wheelchair and my obvious disability."

If there is one element common to all the pets-for-the-handicapped organizations—and, indeed, common to all our relationships with our household pets—it is our old friend, communication. I keep reiterating how communicating with one's pets . . . talking to them . . . is important because so much can be gained by taking advantage of that marvelously attentive sounding board looking up at you. To quote Alamo Reaves of Handi-Dogs, "We haven't *begun* to tap the ability of dogs."

*   *   *

There is a man by the name of Chuck Eisenmann who has carried this business of communicating with animals to a remarkable degree. I think his story is pertinent here, because, although we have been discussing the training of pets for the handicapped, Chuck makes it clear that properly trained pets can enrich all our lives.

Chuck, a professional animal trainer, works with four or five German shepherds at a time, and over the years has performed on innumerable shows. His leader dog, London, even had his own television series in Canada at one time. When I first met Chuck, it was again in connection with our program, *The Pet Set*. We had heard about these sensational trained dogs, and I wanted to check them out, to see if they would be right for our show.

Chuck brought London and Hobo and Raura and Venus to our office. They all walked in—no leashes, of course—and in a small office that was a *lot* of German shepherds! My first impression was that they were so gorgeous that they didn't have to *do* anything. Silly me.

While we spoke with Chuck, the dogs cased the office once over lightly, then went to lie down at one side of the room. Without changing the conversational tone of his voice, Chuck said, "Don't you find it a little dark in here, Hobo? Would you be so kind as to give us a little more illumination?"

In an office he'd never seen before, Hobo got up, walked over and stood up against the wall . . . lightly so as not to scratch . . . and hit the wall switch with his nose. This was just for openers!

Dogs are reputed to see everything in shades of gray, so distinguishing colors is not their best thing. I happened to be wearing a yellow scarf in my hair, and Chuck said, again very offhandedly, "London, would you please show us something inanimate that is the same color as the scarf Betty is wearing?"

Now London had never seen Betty before in his life, and there were two other people in the room. He walked over, carefully put his paws on the arm of my chair, touched the scarf with his nose, then went over and touched a yellow ash tray on Allen's desk. Do I have to add that Chuck and his friends were on our next *two* shows?

Chuck swore that London, his oldest, had a vocabulary of five thousand words and four languages, and who am I to argue? I have long since given up on trying to detect any trick or signal to the dogs from Chuck. There simply isn't any.

Sometimes even Chuck is surprised by the dog's intelligence. Allen and I were so intrigued with this wonderful group that we wanted to share them with our good buddies, Grant Tinker and Mary Tyler Moore (at that time married to each other). One night when Mary and Grant were over, we asked Chuck to stop by with the dogs. This time the potential distractions were compounded—a strange house, strange dog scents (we had four at this point), four adults, and, oh yes, a very noisy blue parakeet named Woodstock.

After our initial greetings, it was time to put the kids on. In his usual low-key fashion, Chuck suggested to London, "Could you show us something inanimate that is the same color as the feathered object in the cage?"

By now, I knew what Chuck was going for—a small figurine of two blue parakeets on a nearby table.

The other three dogs didn't budge as London meandered over to touch Woodstock's cage with his nose. Allen and I were smugly watching Mary and Grant, as London headed for the little china birds on the table. But London passed them by with barely a glance and went on to put his paws carefully on the wall and touch a needlepoint picture hanging there. It was one I'd done long ago of a large *blue* macaw! The most shocked person in the room was Chuck

Eisenmann, who had seen the figurine but not the needle-point.

How can one equate Chuck's miracle dogs with the animals that have been trained to work with the handicapped? It is all a matter of developing potential.

Chuck has some very definite views on the subject. He points out that dogs reflect the attitudes of the people they live with. If we have confidence in our dogs, they will do their best with what they have been taught. He says simply, "Give your dog the same respect you would give another member of the family . . . no less and no more."

Tom Sullivan, in his book *I Am Special,* refers to being blind. He says, "I've learned that dependence is incomprehensible, and independence is impossible; that there must be some level called interdependence."

Well, Tom, your Dinah, and Sharona and Puffin and Mog and Abdul, and all the others like them, are giving all they have toward achieving just that—interdependence.

6.

Rx: One Loving Animal

Let me tell you about Billy. Eight years old, Billy underwent six leg operations. His leg failed to heal properly, and making matters worse, both Billy and his mother seemed to be giving up hope.

"I am going to prescribe a medicine that will surprise you," his doctor announced to the mother one day. "I want you to go out and get a puppy. It will do you both good."

A little mongrel with big funny ears, a moist black nose, huge paws, and brown eyes (guaranteed to pass the audition) was found for Billy, and her presence was felt immediately. For the first time in weeks, Billy laughed. He named his puppy Brownie Gal, and stroked her and combed her and cuddled her in his arms.

The little dog allowed both Billy and his mother to divert their attention from his injured leg, and at long last, the limb began to heal. As the doctor later reported, "The dog was helping the whole family get out of themselves." And Brownie Gal was actually knitting them closer together.

One morning a few weeks later, Billy struggled to his feet and asked for his crutches. "I've got to learn to do this," he explained, "because Brownie Gal needs me to walk her."

Billy's case did not happen just yesterday. It was reported in the March 1960 issue of *Today's Health* magazine. Little, if any, actual scientific evidence existed at that time regarding the therapeutic use of pets. John Beck, then director of the Ellen Prince Speyer Hospital for Animals in New York, was quoted in the article, calling for such documentation. "We are beginning to think that it helps many sick people (and many lonely people) just to have something that is alive. The presence of other life seems to be a stimulus that we need to find out more about."

To illustrate further, Beck recounted the story of a young man who had visited the Speyer Hospital looking for a pet. It seems the man had recently broken up with his family and friends, had developed a bad skin rash, and was becoming very despondent. He thought a pet might help. Beck matched the young man with Uncle Jim, a twenty-four-year-old equally despondent parrot whose original owner had just died. Within two weeks both man and bird were on the mend. The young man's spirits seemed much brighter and his rash had disappeared. The parrot, now talking a blue streak, was supplying the companionship that the man needed so desperately.

"But further," Beck reported, "the parrot supplied dependency. This man needed someone to depend on him. Something good seems to happen to us when someone depends on us."

That, again, was in 1960. Unfortunately, not much more scientific documentation has materialized since then concerning the social benefits of the human/animal bond. The present focus on the subject will at least result in gathering together the wealth of scattered evidence for comparison, evaluation, and subsequent validation. With this data available, a physician can prescribe an appropriate pet under certain circumstances.

Caution, however, must be used with prescription pets just as with any medical procedure, surgery, or drug therapy—to ensure the *right* animal for the given situation. A mistake in judgment can result in aggravating the original problem. In one instance, a psychologist presented his patient, a young man in his twenties suffering from severe depression and low self-image, with an Irish setter puppy as a "new, positive interest." Lack of foresight (and simple common sense) on the psychologist's part—a hyperactive young dog, given to a troubled young man who was away at work all day, from an apartment with no yard—spelled disaster. When the boy, with no alternative, had to give up the dog he had grown fond of, he was left with the feeling he'd failed, and his self-image dropped to a new low; this was a totally unnecessary negative result.

Used with good judgment, a case-history data bank could furnish a profile of the needs of the individual patient . . . and some future Billy could be matched with just the right Brownie Gal, not by luck but by prescription.

Even without the charts and graphs as unimpeachable "proof," many fine programs have been launched during the past twenty years that bring people and animals together. This is particularly true in regimens designed to help the handicapped. The four-legged creatures used here are not exactly *assistance* animals . . . at least not in the same sense that guide dogs assist the blind, or hearing dogs assist the deaf; but like little Billy's Brownie Gal, and especially like the young man's parrot, Uncle Jim, these animals offer their human associates new experiences that reinforce their self-worth and self-esteem.

We do not always think of horses in the same category as dogs and cats, but during the past thirty years, more and more of the country's 8.4 million horses are now considered *companion* animals as opposed to *work* horses. Urban planning now includes "green belts" or parkland, where city dwellers can maintain and ride their own horses. A great indication of the trend toward pet-horse ownership is the 4-H Horse Program whose enrollment has increased sixfold in ten years.

Here again, the bond between horse and human is being extended and used to help those with major health problems.

Riding has become recognized as one of the most beneficial forms of recreational therapy available to the handicapped, particularly children. Psychologically, riding helps develop all the important "selfs"—self-awareness, self-confidence, and self-discipline—as well as improved concentration. One good reason given for this is probably the best: Can you imagine the feelings of someone who has always looked up at the world from a wheelchair or a bed, suddenly elevated to a position *above* his surroundings? From the back of a horse he can look *down,* perhaps for the first time in his life.

I am reminded of the story of an elephant that had a friend who was a flea that rode around behind his ear. One day they crossed a jungle bridge that swayed pendulously. After crossing the bridge, the flea whispered into the elephant's ear, "We sure shook that bridge, didn't we?"

The feeling a handicapped rider receives when placed on a horse is much the same. The rider, however, has one advantage over the flea—he is in control. Having been a patient under the care of someone else, he now has in his own hands the reins through which this enormous animal beneath him will follow *his* directions.

Jean Baeum, executive director of the Heartland School of Riding in Overland Park, Kansas, puts it this way, "A rider who cannot walk is able to run on the strong legs of his horse. The mentally retarded can learn to ride, and ride quite well. The horse is patient; he allows the rider to learn slowly. An emotionally troubled rider can achieve control and friendship. The horse is warm and friendly; he will not turn away." And writer Beverly Blume adds, "To children and adults who feel 'different' from their peers, the nonjudgmental affection and loyalty of an animal makes all the difference in the world."

Physically, riding strengthens and relaxes muscles, improves posture, balance, and coordination, and increases joint mobility. For those in wheelchairs who have no natural means of locomotion, the action of the horse—the up-and-down and side-to-side movement—builds muscle tone while diverting the interest of the individual; it alleviates the deadly boredom of regular therapeutic exercises.

All physically disabled people are not able to participate in an activity of this kind, but a surprising number can and do. Each potential rider undergoes a careful evaluation by his physician, his physical therapist, and a trained riding instructor. *All* riding exercises are not appropriate for *all* students, depending on the nature of the disability. A child whose joints are fused cannot flex his foot to get his heels down in the stirrups, but he is able to participate in certain riding exercises that can strengthen other parts of his body.

Therapeutic riding is used in *addition* to regular therapy, never in place of treatment the student may be already receiving, and it should always be used in close interchange with medical advisors. This is vital, for, in the last analysis, it will be the medical profession which will bestow the all-important stamp of approval on the use of riding for therapy.

The first documented use of therapeutic horseback riding was by Chassigne, in Paris. As far back as 1875, it was he who used riding to treat neurological disorders. Improved balance and muscle control were reported, as well as a marked improvement in patient morale.

Chassigne must have been well ahead of his time, for it has only been in the last thirty years that there has been renewed interest in the idea of teaming horses and the handicapped. It was a woman named Liz Hartel, in Copenhagen, who first showed the world what could be accomplished. She rode in the 1952 Olympic Games in Helsinki and won a silver medal in dressage. Not many women had ever achieved such a victory, but Ms. Hartel's achievement was particularly satisfying—Liz had been a polio victim.

"She showed it could be done," says Virginia Martin of Borderland Farm in Warwick, New York. "Before that, everyone thought that handicapped persons could not ride. After Helsinki, a movement started in Europe . . . years before being thought of in this country."

By 1953, a Mrs. Norah Jacques had started a riding program in England for two spastic children. From this modest beginning, her interest grew to the extent that she later founded the Pony Riding for the Disabled Trust, the largest school in Western Europe, leading to similar schools in England and throughout the continent.

The Diamond Riding Center for the Handicapped is such a school, founded in the late 1960's to provide riding for the urban handicapped of South London. Within only a few years, the center was serving an average of seven hundred riders a week throughout the year. Keith Webb, founder of the center, believes very highly in its usefulness: "Riding a pony gives the handicapped the opportunity for nonverbal communication and for emotional expression. The pony accepts them as they are and does not make patronizing concessions for their disability. The freedom of movement that the pony gives brings freedom of physical expression denied to many of them. Imagine the freedom of movement that the pony gives the blind! The handicapped all have a right to take their place in society. If two legs cannot get them there, then perhaps four good legs of a pony can."

Webb mentions a boy named John, a spastic child whose malady, John's father alleged, had driven the boy's mother to commit suicide. After being abandoned by his father, the sensitive child was turned over to the local authorities and withdrew more and more from life around him. His one love was animals, so the social workers handling his case enrolled him at the Diamond Riding Center . . . and little by little the boy came out of his shell. Before he left the program, it was John who was leading the festivities at the school's public exhibitions, clearing jumps that longtime sportsmen might refuse. "The cheers and applause that followed," Webb recalls, "would have been envied by any international jumper."

The accomplishments of the handicapped in riding programs have proven to have a ripple effect, benefiting other members of the riders' families. "We all need to feel a sense of pride in the achievements of those nearest and dearest to us," Webb reminds us. "The opportunities open to the parents of a mentally handicapped child are few and far between." Therefore, each of Webb's riders receives periodic certificates attesting to his individual level of proficiency. These testimonials are as satisfying to many parents as any other "good report card." Webb remembers one student who was severely mentally impaired and could accomplish only so much. But this lad, too, received a certificate. It stated the truth: "Paul has ridden for five years and loves his horse very much." Paul's family was very proud.

Formal therapeutic riding programs did not really get under way on this side of the Atlantic until 1968. Prior to this, in the early 1920's, intermittent projects were operated by various individuals, most notably in Canada. But as with many of the other programs for the handicapped, it was the late 1960's before the general public recognized a real value in riding for the disabled. And then, as if making up for lost time, local riding centers started appearing all over the map.

The aforementioned Virginia Martin began working with the handicapped at her Borderland Farm at about that time. "I had some friends with brain-damaged children," she recalls, "and I put them in with my regular riders." She has been working with the disabled ever since.

That same year, 1968, Maudie-Hunter Warfel founded Happy Horsemanship for the Handicapped near Philadelphia, and Mr. and Mrs. Dean Bedford started working with a group of children in Maryland. But perhaps the real turning point came in January 1970, when the Cheff Center in Augusta, Michigan, opened its doors under the leadership of Lida L. McCowan, conceded to be the foremost authority on therapeutic riding in this country today.

Lida, born in the heart of horse country—Glencoe, Maryland—has been riding since the age of five, when her father bought her a Shetland-Welsh pony. By the time she was eight, she was riding in fox hunts, and when she reached the ripe old age of ten, she got her first Thoroughbred.

By the mid-1960's, Lida, by now herself a mother of five, was directing Sterling Farms Riding School and Camp in West Virginia. She had had gratifying results working with one boy with cerebral palsy and another with mental retardation, but the vast majority of her students were not disabled. She was rather overwhelmed, therefore, when the Cheff Foundation approached her to head up its new project, an equestrian center for the disabled. Overwhelmed or not, Lida was never one to turn down a worthwhile challenge. She headed to England to study with John Davies, the leading British authority; upon her return, Lida helped design the Cheff facility and has been its guiding spirit ever since.

Today the Cheff Center is recognized as the world's largest school built exclusively to teach riding to the handicapped, with more than two hundred mentally and/or physically disabled youths participating in classes each week. "I've worked with 'normal' students for years," Lida says, "and I'll take these young people anytime. Their ded-

ication and determination is inspiring . . . they want so
badly to do well."

Listening to the people Tom and I contacted, who
work with the handicapped, in whatever fields, one is
struck by the consistency in attitude. There is an unmistak-
able sense of sheer uncondescending joy. One young
trainer from Cheff was addressing a group of us and seriously explaining her involvement in the program. Suddenly, as if it bubbled up from deep inside, she smiled and
interrupted herself to say, "I just *love* these people . . .
they always give the very best they can."

The center, of course, makes no promises. "We do our
best," Lida continues, "but we have no miracle cures here.
Riding isn't for everyone, just as tennis or swimming isn't.
We do have some striking success stories. But we can't help
everyone."

Lida McCowan's students all suffer from some impair-
ment. Some are unable to walk, others to see, still others to
hear. Some are unable to respond rationally in simple circumstances. Some seem unable to love or even listen. That,
at least, is the prognosis at the time they are enrolled at
Cheff. Most of them change. "As a class, I think it's the
physically handicapped child . . . five to fourteen . . . who
benefits most from the riding therapy. They too often have
no other group activities. While they're here, they compete
with others in their age groupings who have the same types
of disabilities. As a class, the multiple handicapped . . .
physical and mental . . . probably receive the least benefit.
Occasionally, however, one'll surprise us and make remarkable progress."

For some, whose disabilities preclude actual riding,
driving a cart is an alternative. They are still in contact with
the horse.

The Cheff Center is but one of the 160 centers for

therapeutic riding currently in operation in the United States and Canada. About half of these have been accredited by an organization called NARHA, the North American Riding for the Handicapped Association. Lida McCowan and Alexander Mackay-Smith created NARHA in 1969 to set standards of uniformity and excellence for the many new programs getting under way. To achieve accreditation from NARHA, a riding center must meet and maintain high standards in regard to safety, horses, volunteer workers, trained instructors, lesson plans and procedures, equipment, facilities—all the variables that go into a safe, humane, effective equestrian program.

Students at Cheff Center not only learn good horsemanship skills, they get to utilize what they've learned by playing games. Instructors turn exercise sessions into friendly contests whenever possible. Such activities keep the children alert, yet relaxed and confident, and often provide a new learning opportunity. What's more, it allows them to forget that they are actually in this class for therapy (they must grow to dislike that word) and, once again, boring exercises become exciting encounters.

While never losing sight of the seriousness of their goals, Cheff instructors try to keep the atmosphere of the center light. As one employee puts it, "I think it's important around these kids to have an atmosphere of fun. There is too much seriousness around them all the time. The high spirits generated by the people who work here kind of spill over into these kids. They love to come out here."

Informality, a tone set at the top by Lida McCowan, filters all the way down to the students. Jokes, teasing, even good-natured insults, all keep the spirits high. "We don't baby them," insists Lida about her students. "If one falls on a hall floor, we're liable to say, 'Hey, you just hurt that floor!'" Such a comment may elicit laughter from the child, or an equally clever remark, but one thing's for sure—the child won't just sit there feeling sorry for himself.

In 1976, eight Cheff students, all mentally retarded, rode in the International Special Olympics at Mount Pleasant, Michigan. The group not only had the honor of leading the parade of 3,300 athletes into the stadium, they performed drills, exhibitions and games. Spectators and officials were so impressed that riding was subsequently added to all Special Olympics events. Lida is especially proud to report that some of the students have competed successfully in events against nonhandicapped riders.

But smaller personal successes count, too. "We had one little autistic girl," Lida explains, "who never said a word. One day we found her in the barn with the pony she rode. She was patting him and saying, 'Nice pony, nice pony.' And these things happen all the time. It's what makes it so worthwhile."

While attributing the success of the Cheff Center to the skills of the instructors and volunteers, Lida candidly admits, "The horses are the real heroes here." She recalls the time a child fell off a horse into the soft sod of the arena and landed right under one of the horse's front feet . . . which was in midair. "The horse froze instantly with his foot lifted!" Lida remembers. "He stood there the whole fifteen seconds it took for us to reach the child and lift her. Then he put his foot down. *The horses know!* I swear they understand that these people need special care."

"No," she continues, "any one of us could go and they wouldn't miss us. But take away the horses and you have no program."

Tom and I saw all this in action when we attended the annual meeting of NARHA in Pomona, California. Watching the pride and pleasure they take in the work they do, it's little wonder that they achieve such fine results.

The president of NARHA, Maria Kyne, agrees that the real therapist is the four-legged one. For this reason, the selection of mounts for therapeutic programs is of the utmost importance, and the requirements are clearly drawn.

The prime requisite is *temperament*, since the safety of the student is, of course, top priority.

Size is a real consideration. Some students, because of their disability, are not able to straddle a large, barrel-chested horse, and they also may be intimidated by too large an animal. In addition, with beginners, or in some instances where balance is a problem, helpers walk alongside and must be able to reach up to a rider in need of assistance.

Gait should be as smooth as possible, but there should be three distinct gaits so a student can learn to distinguish and cope with a horse's change of pace.

Age range is very broad, as long as the horse is not too young to be reliable or too old to be durable.

The *sex* of the animal is not a prime concern. Stallions, of course, would not be considered. Otherwise, while geldings are probably the preference, a mare, in many cases, seems to have an uncanny understanding of the handicapped youngster on her back.

Once a horse meets all those qualifications, *then* he is ready to be trained to cope with the unusual things he will encounter with his young riders: Mounting ramps mustn't spook him, nor wheelchairs, nor crutches, nor clanking walking frames. He must get used to being mounted from either side. At times he will have an inexperienced rider on his back, with a side walker—perhaps two—accompanying his every step around the ring.

Horses have good memories, especially of things they *don't* like, so the indoctrination of a new horse is kept as low-key and pleasant as possible. Older, more experienced horses can be invaluable in calming jumpy animals new to the job. Eventually, the horses learn to stand rock-still no matter what is going on around them.

Voice has a tremendous significance in this type of endeavor. The horse must respond immediately to sharp voice commands, particularly if any difficulties should arise. In this one respect, the response is much like that of a circus horse.

It is not all work and no play for these gentle giants. They, too, must have a period of R and R. To break the routine, a horse must be ridden regularly by an able rider. Turning him out now and then, to play and kick up his heels in a shaded pasture, will keep him from going stale.

In dealing with the variety of health problems presented by the students, Maria Kyne says the instructor needs a high level of self-confidence, particularly with the mentally handicapped, since these people are super-perceptive. They have a short attention span and can be quick to anger as well as to pick up on any favoritism. An instructor's basic teaching skills are amplified to meet the challenge. Another caution: Never generalize . . . keep eyes on each individual.

The students have a deep need to succeed, so it is important to set them up for success. What you expect is what you get. A series of exercises must not be too difficult yet must still present a challenge. And the instructor must be firm . . . fair . . . short . . . and consistent.

At Cheff there are six volunteers working with blind riders. Before the children begin to ride, they "feel" the horse all over, while an instructor explains. They will also—many times—feel the face of the instructor, so they are no longer strangers. The choice of mount for these riders is even more special.

Lida tells of an emotionally disturbed blind boy who, in *three weeks,* was riding. It was interesting to hear Lida differentiate between those born blind and those who have lost their sight more recently. The latter, she says, tend to be angry and a little more difficult to reach, while those who have always been without sight seem to add the other four senses up to make a "sixth."

A classic example of that quality is one Marcia Springston Jennings. Blind since birth, Marcia, with her older sister, also blind, managed a professional barn, training and showing horses for many years. She's still at it. And she didn't choose just any breed of horse . . . she chose the hot headed Arabian!

Marcia, like Tom Sullivan, knows that those who have always been blind have a specialized sense of "feel," and they can actually *hear* obstacles in their path. She does not recommend trying to teach this sixth sense to those who have lost their sight, having once been able to see. Marcia says it is something they must find for themselves, since trying to learn it from someone else can be frustrating to the point of self-defeat.

Frances Joswick, instructor and NARHA board member, emphasized that to make the mistake of being patronizing with these young people is a real turnoff. Innovation is welcome as long as it suits the capabilities of the students. She said there are really only two ironclad rules: Is it safe? Is it humane?

Frances even hangs a punching bag in the stable so a youngster can work off his frustration and let off steam before he communicates these feelings to his mount.

The important ingredient in riding for therapy is team effort. The horse and rider are a *team* working together. The horse is the reward for all the painstaking hard work and good behavior. Mounts and volunteers are changed rather frequently as a rule, to avoid too strong an attachment to one horse or one helper. This builds confidence so that a child grows to trust other horses . . . other people . . . and eventually him- or herself.

Here in Southern California, the *Real People* television

program brought national attention to another equine-assisted therapy program. Ahead With Horses is now in its fifteenth year and has a completely different approach. This facility, managed by Liz and Lew Helms, specializes in teaching *vaulting*—that is, gymnastics on horseback. Included in their classes are children—anywhere from 60 to 130 per week—plus a few adults, suffering from any number of handicaps—cerebral palsy, autism, Down's syndrome, mental retardation, multiple sclerosis. Liz told us many of her students come to them as a last resort, after having run up a long list of failures in other programs. She feels, however, that it is often the most severely handicapped individuals who have taught the instructors many secrets of the human/animal bond.

Vaulting—a sport that dates back more than two thousand years to the arenas of ancient Rome—is similar in nature to gymnastics performed today on a mat (always a popular event when we watch the Olympic Games on television). The horse, then, is in a sense used like a prop, as no actual "riding" is involved.

Each lesson is designed to promote advancement in motor development, language, and social behavior. Off the horse, the students learn grooming and stable management . . . plus a few subjects they may have missed out on in "normal" schools. Primary reading, writing, and arithmetic skills are often worked into lesson plans and, of course, are couched in "horse-related" terms.

Ahead With Horses also sponsors the Woodcraft Ranger Program, which is essentially a handicapped child's equivalent of the Boy and Girl Scouts. This youth achievement program, again built around horses, teaches leadership, citizenship, and ecology.

The overall philosophy at AWH is to create productive independence for the students. Positive images are stressed; "I can't" is not acceptable. All schools teach about President

Franklin Roosevelt; AWH teaches that the man was both President and handicapped. "I can!"

Hoping to curb some of the social stigmas that the students have picked up elsewhere, AWH has its own vernacular. A wheelchair, for example, is called a "chariot" and likened to the glorious two-wheel racers of Rome. Children with body braces are called "bionic vaulters," and taught the wonders of such modern hardware.

While never exposing the child to danger, Ahead With Horses, unlike other programs, allows handicapped horses to participate in the classes. The students call these steeds "recycled animals," just as they themselves are "recycled people." Seeing that a horse who is totally blind can still function and make a contribution to life allows the handicapped youngster to believe that he too can find a place for himself.

The grounds have also become a home for a few cats and dogs, all of whom appear to have been mistreated or abandoned at some earlier stage of their lives. Again, these animals and the children seem to have an affinity for each other. The youngsters are often more afraid of these little animals than of the big horses, and the recently arrived dogs and cats likewise approach these new human friends tentatively. Before long, however, both sides mellow, and great friendships are formed. Both the smaller animals and the horses seem to sense that the handicapped are special and allow the children to hold and touch and try their patience in ways they would never tolerate from the rest of us.

It was in the spring of 1982 that *Real People* aired a segment concerning Ahead With Horses. It was a story about Chad Saphro, a young boy who had been helped a great deal through his experience with AWH.

In Apache Junction, Arizona, another young man, ten-year-old Sam Edwards, watched that show with his mother. Sam had cerebral palsy and was so badly crippled, physically, there was little hope of improvement. He and his mother felt that Ahead With Horses was their only hope and vowed to do anything to get his chance in California. The entire town of Apache Junction pitched in. They had bake sales, cook-offs, sewing bees . . . and they raised four thousand dollars. With one goal in mind, Mrs. Edwards left her husband and brought Sam to Liz Helms. All that determination is paying off. Sam's coordination improved, his speech improved, and above all, so did his outlook on life.

We have used the words handicapped and disabled again and again in these pages. There will be those who may quarrel with the terms. One person I read recently does not like the word "handicap," saying it conjures up the ancient picture of the crippled beggar in the street proffering his "handy cap" for charity. Someone else takes exception to the word "special," insisting that the disabled are the same as everyone else. Another suggestion is to capitalize the last half of "disABLED" to make it more positive.

The semantics are unimportant. I don't believe for one minute that these people we've been talking about are the same as anyone else. They have a drive and a determination and an appreciation of the positives that is unmatched. The rest of us *could* consider lack of those qualities our handicap.

Lida McCowan said it all in the title of her book: *It's Ability That Counts.*

Pet-visiting day at a nursing home near Pullman, Washington, brings smiles and love to all concerned . . . (COURTESY OF PEOPLE-PET PARTNERSHIP PROGRAM)

. . . as it does at the Beverly Manor Convalescent Home, near my house in Carmel, California. (PHOTOGRAPH BY FLOSSIE STOWELL)

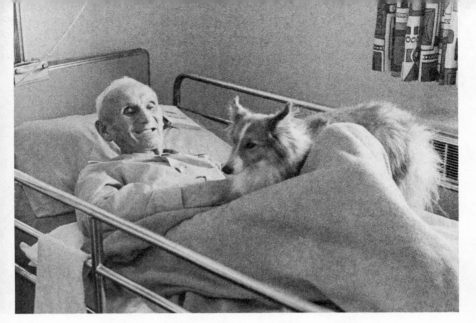

Even in bed, convalescing patients get cheery visits from this sheltie at a nursing home in Moscow, Idaho. (COURTESY OF PEOPLE-PET PARTNERSHIP PROGRAM)

Pullman (Wash.) schoolchildren learn about the care of a guinea pig through the People-Pet Partnership Program. (COURTESY OF PEOPLE-PET PARTNERSHIP PROGRAM)

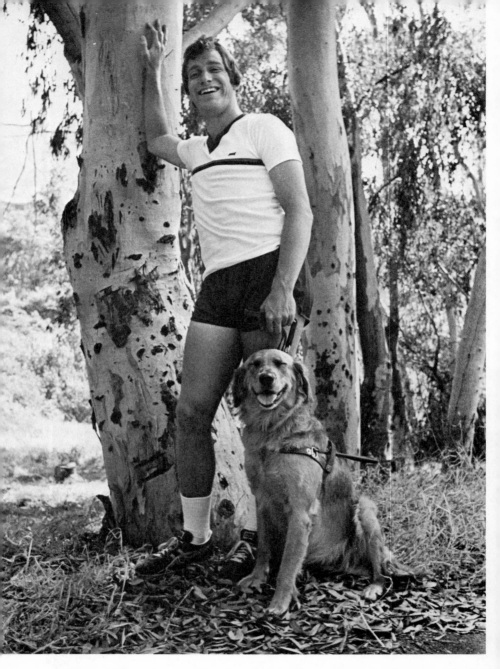

Actor, author, singer, golfer, parachutist, skier, motorcyclist, horseman, jogger Tom Sullivan and his guide dog, Dinah. (PHOTOGRAPH BY STEVE SCHATZBERG; COURTESY OF TOM SULLIVAN)

Darryl Anderson ("Animal" on TV's *Lou Grant*) devotes much of his time to working with hearing-ear dogs.
(COURTESY OF AMERICAN HUMANE ASSOCIATION)

Dr. Leo Bustad, dean of the College of Veterinary Medicine, Washington State University, playfully calls Bridgette, his wife's hearing-ear dog, "Dingbat."
(COURTESY OF PEOPLE-PET PARTNERSHIP PROGRAM)

This hearing-ear dog watches over baby and alerts the rest of the household when the child cries . . .

. . . while this fellow wakes his mistress at the ringing of her alarm . . . or at any number of other sounds. (COURTESY OF AMERICAN HUMANE ASSOCIATION)

Alamo "Bitsy" Reaves's Handi-Dog, Mog, brings her her crutches.
(PHOTOGRAPH BY BARBARA TELLMAN; COURTESY OF ALAMO REAVES)

Lillie Passano, ninety-six, trainer and graduate of Handi-Dogs, credits her companions, Yin and Yang, with saving her life. (COURTESY OF ALAMO REAVES)

Therapeutic riding has given a whole new perspective to the handicapped.
(COURTESY OF LEONARD WARNER)

This sheltie, one of the dogs in the Prison Partnership Program, is learning to fetch items, such as these eyeglasses, for a disabled owner. (COURTESY OF WASHINGTON STATE UNIVERSITY)

Purdy's Prison Partnership Program: Coordinator Kathy Quinn, center, trainer Marsha Hinkel, far right, and their inmate volunteers. (COURTESY OF KATHY QUINN)

A pygmy goat is but one of the animals used in David Lee's pet-therapy program at Lima State Hospital. (COURTESY OF DAVID LEE)

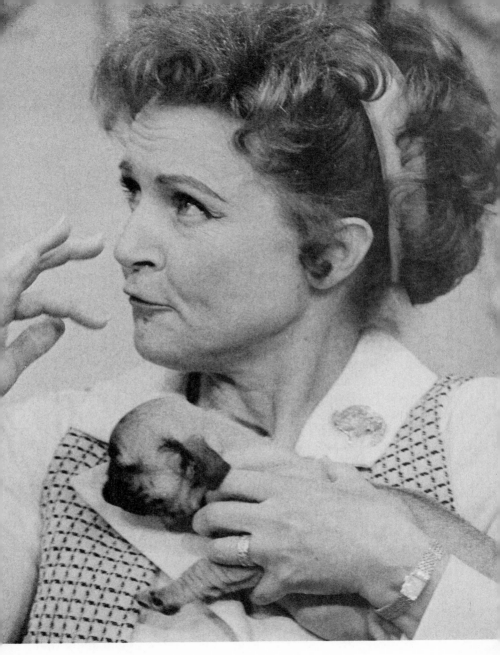

The human/animal bond . . . like mother, like son?

7.

My Pet, My Therapist

During the Second World War, as we have mentioned, the Army Air Force Convalescent Center in Pawling, New York, was the first in this country to experiment with what has since been labeled "pet-facilitated psychotherapy." It all began when one particular Pawling patient, a lieutenant who was scheduled to be at the center for some time, started asking publicly about securing a dog as a pet. The American Red Cross found a beautiful German shepherd puppy named Fritz, and a man working at the center, who had had experience with the Air Force Canine Corps, agreed to help train and care for the dog. According to what few reports still exist, "Fritz did wonders for the officer patient. The lieutenant developed increased security, ambition, and interest through his feeling of responsibility in having a dog to care for, and through the dog's immediate devotion to his new master."

The center's success with Fritz produced an avalanche of requests for pets from other patients, and an entire program was initiated and continued for the duration of the war.

Now, forty years later, scientists are coming to "rediscover" the secret of Fritz. Dr. James Lynch feels that "there is a biological need, reflected in our hearts, to form

loving relationships. . . . Animals cannot take the place of
another human being, but they are another important di-
mension through which the need for companionship may be
satisfied."

As we have discussed in the previous chapters, pets
and animals of every kind are being purposely introduced
into therapeutic settings with the physically and emotionally handicapped. While the success vs. failure rate is
much easier to compute with the physically disabled—say,
a blind person's interaction with his guide dog—psychologists and psychiatrists have witnessed some remarkable
successes with pets and the *emotionally* impaired.

This whole notion of mixing animals with psychotherapy is, of course, far more controversial than using assistance animals with the physically disabled, where results
are more tangible, and is anything but universally accepted
today. More and more practitioners are, however, slowly
introducing pets into their practice settings.

Dr. Aline Kidd relates the story of a little boy who
would not talk and was sent to her for treatment. He arrived at her office, proceeded to curl himself into a ball,
pulled his jacket over his head, and wrote a note, "Leave
me alone!" The boy's mother indicated that he communi-
cated only with his cat, so the doctor encouraged her to
bring the cat along on the next visit. She recalled the experience later: "This was a giant male cat, one torn ear, overweight, scarred, ugly. The little boy talked to the cat. I
talked to the cat. In about two months the boy began to
talk to me, because I talked to the cat."

Several times I had occasion to visit patients in the
neuropsychiatric ward at the UCLA Medical Center. This
particular area was under tight security, but once inside the
locked doors, the patients were free to mingle in the day
rooms. A tiny parakeet was the mascot of this particular

facility, and he could always be found flying, unrestricted, from room to room. Several patients made a special point of introducing me to him, sometimes repeatedly; the nurse told me he could always be counted on as a popular and safe subject through which the patients could communicate with each other. I couldn't help but notice that a couple of the more withdrawn young people never took their eyes from this tiny beautiful creature.

Then there is the case of Sonny, a nineteen-year-old psychotic who spent most of his time lying in a hospital bed in mummy position. Nothing the staff tried—from recreational therapy to drugs—seemed to alter his withdrawn and totally uncommunicative behavior. Prior to administering electroshock treatments, Sonny's doctors decided to try pet therapy. A little wirehaired fox terrier named Arwyn was placed on the young man's bed and immediately jumped on Sonny and licked his face and ears. The boy, to everyone's surprise, burst out in grins from ear to ear, raised himself up on one elbow, and volunteered his first question: "Where can I keep him?" The psychiatrists on the case credit Arwyn with creating the initial breakthrough that ultimately led to Sonny's recovery.

The key to the story lies in two words in this last sentence: *initial breakthrough.* Where problems are so complex and deep-seated, pets cannot and should not be expected to execute permanent personality change. However, if pet therapy can help open that locked door and make a patient reachable . . . provide that initial breakthrough . . . the program has earned its keep.

Child psychologist Boris Levinson puts it this way: "Using a pet is not an open sesame to the 'inner world' of the mentally disturbed." He adds that when pets do help, "the progress is at best very slow. However, clinical evidence indicates that having a pet does speed up therapy and a relationship is established much sooner."

Levinson knows whereof he speaks. He is perhaps the world's foremost proponent of pet-facilitated psychotherapy, having incorporated pets, particularly his own dog, Jingles, into therapy sessions since the mid-fifties. His books, *Pet-Oriented Child Psychotherapy* and *Pets and Human Development,* are recognized as the first important texts to be published on the subject.

At that time Dr. Levinson was, along with Jingles, blazing a trail through uncharted territory. He certainly did not set out with the idea of using Jingles as a co-therapist; it happened quite unintentionally when a woman and her very disturbed little boy arrived at his door one day, hours early for an appointment. As a rule, Jingles would be excluded from the office during consultations, but this was unexpected. The little boy immediately made contact with the dog, cuddling and petting him. By the end of the visit the child indicated that he wanted to come back to see the dog. It was the beginning of successful therapy for the boy, and the start of a fourteen-year career as a co-therapist for Jingles.

Dr. Levinson's theories about pets for use in psychotherapy are based on the premise that it may be easier for the child to project or share his feelings with a pet than with an adult, and also on the animal's ability to fulfill some of the child's need for cuddling, companionship, and unconditional acceptance.

Not appropriate for all situations, pets have been used by Dr. Levinson very selectively. When added to a therapy session, however, a pet has been seen to supply the child with an opportunity to feel "the master of the situation." A troubled child's need for affection is well met by a pet who does not scold and does not expect the child always to be on his best behavior. Indeed, troubled youngsters learn that pets will not desert them or laugh at them or send them away. The pet's love is constant. Once a pet-child rapport is established, children are often able to transfer feelings of trust from the pet to the therapist, to the parents, and finally, to others.

Dr. Levinson introduced his methodology for pet-oriented psychotherapy in 1961 at an Annual Convention of the American Psychological Association, in a speech that was met with everything from guffaws to skepticism to genuine interest. Happily, people with the latter reaction had the most stamina, and today the field of animal/human relationships is respected as an area worthy of legitimate scientific investigation. "The problem of mental disorders in children is so vast," Dr. Levinson maintains, "any plausible measure that promises diminution deserves investigation and testing."

Dr. Michael McCulloch echoes the sentiment: "If pet therapy offers hope for relief of human suffering, then it is our professional obligation to explore every available avenue for its use."

Perhaps the most baffling mental disorders are those that render the patient withdrawn and uncommunicative. One of the most heart rending is infantile autism. Dr. Levinson explains, "For them the world never existed, is dead, or no longer exists. They are the only ones left alive. As a result, they frequently create an imaginary world with imaginary companions. When there is a cherished pet nearby, it may bring a ray of reality into this child's world."

Liz Helms's Ahead With Horses program has had marked success with a couple of autistic students. One young man, whom we shall call Miguel, came to the program two years ago, at age seven. He had no language skills (other than being able to "echo" back, like a parrot, a few words), no affectionate responses for family or friends, no advanced motor skills (he couldn't hop, skip, jump, or run), no motivation for learning.

Miguel was referred to Liz by a major Los Angeles pediatric hospital, which had essentially done all it could for the lad. The school accepted him on a three-month probationary agreement—to wit, if at the end of three months he had shown any meaningful improvement, a state agency would pay for him to continue classes indefinitely.

Miguel was allowed to choose his own horse, and which did this little guy choose but a super large (seventeen hands, three inches) Appaloosa named Napoleon, a horse that is essentially allowed to roam the grounds free. Associating on his own with this big, beautiful animal, Miguel learned to walk with the horse, to make Napoleon go in a certain direction by touching him in the flank area, even how to make the horse trot.

The day Miguel's three months were up, the lad's parents and representatives of the state agency came and saw him go through various vaulting tests—some successfully, some not—but using one of the other horses. Everyone was debating Miguel's future when suddenly the boy disappeared. Panic! But no, look, there he is now—his little head barely visible in the yellow sea of tall mustard plants growing in the field. Miguel had gone to fetch his friend Napoleon, who was roaming up in the canyon. The lad led Nap, as he's called, back to the central area, put him in the paddock, and locked the gate. The visitors couldn't believe their eyes.

Obviously, Miguel stayed with Ahead With Horses and, in the intervening two years, has learned to communicate in both English and Spanish. At Christmastime last year, he spontaneously gave his mother his first big hug. He's even been helpful in communicating and assisting with the education of other autistic pupils in the program.

Similar success has been noted in recent studies involving dolphins—yes, dolphins—not really in the "pet" classification. In 1978, Henry Truby, director of scientific research for the World Dolphin Foundation; Nancy Phillips, consultant to the South Florida Society for Autistic Children; and Betsy Smith, associate professor of social work at Florida International University (Miami), joined forces in a study to determine whether dolphins might alter the behavior of autistic children. The study included six encounter sessions between eight autistic children and three dolphins.

Reporting the results in *Science News* magazine, writer Joan Arehart-Treichel indicates, "All of the children showed marked prolonged attention spans in the presence of the dolphins, and several showed some other behavior improvements as well."

She tells of one particular eighteen-year-old boy named Michael, who, prior to the study, was known to verbalize only two words—"Dad" and "beer." During the encounter sessions, Michael not only "reached out" from his own immediate environment to help feed the dolphins, but started making clicking sounds to attract the dolphins' attention.

Moreover, Michael exhibited his delight in the dolphins even at home. (Sustained changes in behavior among the autistic are not that common.) He started to notice pictures of dolphins in books, and would make clicking sounds at dolphins in television commercials and billboards. Perhaps most encouraging of all, he said the word "Yep" five times within a single week when asked whether he wanted to go again to visit his new dolphin friends.

There was also a young girl in a dolphin therapy program who imitated their clicking sound so well that the experimenter could not differentiate between girl and dolphin!

Dogs, cats, horses, and dolphins are not the only creatures being used in animal-facilitated psychotherapy sessions. Everything from ants and alligators to frogs and seagulls, snails, lizards, snakes and goldfish are being used in one program or another. The Green Chimneys Farm, a resident school for emotionally disturbed children, in Brewster, New York, has established an entire working farm. Youngsters there raise cows, sheep, horses, pigs, goats, ducks, and chickens—everything you'd expect on a farm. The animals function as part of the special education and therapy the children receive. As author Patricia Curtis explains, "It is believed that the animals, from the powerful horses down to the littlest ducklings and lambs, help the youngsters become more responsible, self-controlled and socialized."

Roger Caras, writing about Green Chimneys for *Science Digest,* included the following vignette:

> One violent, street-smart 11-year-old didn't even know what a rabbit looked like when he arrived at Green Chimneys last year. "Someone had to tell me what that furry animal was," he recalls with a grin. The Farm Center's 4-H chapter changed all that. Hugging his prizewinning angora rabbit, the calm, communicative child told me what it felt like to have cared for his pet and raised it to be a trophy winner in a local show. "It made me feel real good," he said, smiling. "It was the goodest thing that ever happened to me."

Duane W. Christy, executive director, Children's Protective Service of the Ohio Humane Society, has worked for years with children in placement—that is, with children living away from their own families. Writing in *National Humane Review,* Christy says, "Pets—and especially dogs—seem to help children bridge the gap between fantasy and reality." Moreover, he adds, "We found that the dog's dependency forces a child to act positively and to think about something besides himself and his own personal problems."

Other experts agree. While touring the facilities of a psychiatric hospital in Alaska a few years ago, Dr. Leo Bustad was introduced to a large white dog named Princess. "She is the most important member of our therapy staff," admitted the hospital chaplain. Many of the disturbed people there, the chaplain explained, related initially only to the dog.

For the first five and a half years after Allen and I were married, we lived in Westchester County, New York. It is the same county where a school for delinquent boys was founded over a hundred years ago. Lincoln Hall, sprawling over almost a thousand acres, is run by the Christian Brothers, a Roman Catholic teaching order, ably assisted by "social-worker dogs." This came about by accident when a monk took a walk in the moonlight one night and overheard a boy talking to a Russian wolfhound . . . telling him all his troubles. This was the same boy who had refused to utter a word to the school psychiatrist. One of the brothers explained, "Dogs help many of the boys bridge the gap when they first arrive here, hostile, sullen, withdrawn. . . . The boy feels at home with the dog—who seems to him the only living creature who doesn't know and couldn't care less that his newfound friend has run afoul of the law."

"Animals are less threatening than people," says Mira Rothenberg, clinical director of Blueberry Treatment Centers, a network of residences for disturbed children. Dr. Levinson agrees: "Disturbed children often have a strong need for physical contact, but are afraid of human contact because they have been hurt so much and so often by people." Pets provide them with a safe outlet.

So completely did Dr. Levinson believe this concept

that he decided that as an uncontrolled experiment he would leave his precious Jingles at Camp Blueberry for several weeks one summer in the mid-fifties.

By now, Jingles, with many long hours of consultation behind him, had acquired the knack of adapting his personality to the specific needs of each child, something even a highly qualified therapist finds not always possible.

Director Mira Rothenberg reported that Jingles (called "Levinson" by the children) benefited many of the residents, but his biggest victory over the summer was accomplished with a very disturbed child who was deathly afraid of dogs, who would scream if he saw a dog and faint if one brushed by him. With this child Jingles controlled his exuberance . . . never jumping to lick Andy's face, as he did with the other children who loved him . . . but always remaining quietly nearby.

Gradually, Andy grew fascinated and, at last, brave enough to feed and even touch the dog. And when he shouted for "Levinson," the dog would appear from wherever he happened to be and wait patiently by Andy's side.

At summer's end, Jingles returned home to resume his work with Dr. Levinson. The good doctor made the point that Jingles's ability to reach the various children at Camp Blueberry, where other dogs on the property had failed, was more than mere chance. Through his years in a psychologist's office, Jingles had learned to pick up cues from the patients and adapt his behavior accordingly.

While with Jingles it was a case of on-the-job training, Dr. Levinson maintained that it would be feasible to educate adaptable dogs to work with the mentally ill, and that to avoid problems only specially trained dogs should be used.

That was thirty years ago. Just such programs are in progress today.

Jay Meranchik, founder of the Feeling Heart Foundation, a nonprofit organization that takes specially trained dogs into mental institutions and nursing homes on the Eastern Shore of Chesapeake Bay (Maryland), believes the use of dogs able to obey commands is particularly important in pet-therapy programs. He recalls one child who was having serious speech problems: "When she found out that the dog could speak on command, she tried for some twenty or thirty minutes to get the command out. When the word finally came, the dog responded, which egged the child on, until a complete speech pattern was built."

Addressing the Society of Companion-Animal Studies meeting on "Pets and Children," in London in March 1983, Ann Hamlin recalled her experiences on a psychiatric hospital ward with a retired guide dog named Kim:

> Kim was still "illegal" when I had a phone call one snowy day from the Senior Nursing Officer. "I would never believe it, I've just seen Liz playing in the snow with your dog." Liz was a young, very successful professional lady who had been in the hospital for two years. During that time she had been miserable and non-communicative. She frequently mutilated herself, and sat around her ward all day making zero progress.
>
> We can't claim Kim "cured" Liz, but she certainly helped her find an identity as Kim's walker, and one day, was even given the responsibility of accompanying my husband to fetch the dog from the vet and cook scrambled eggs for her!

Then there is the story of Snowball, a small black-and-white dog that lives at Rainier School, a facility for the mentally retarded and multiply handicapped in Buckley, Washington. Snowball was smuggled in by some of the boys, but very quickly became an asset to all the residents.

One of his "masters" is a retarded youth named Randy. John Gaunt, an attendant at the school, recalls that Randy's eighteenth birthday was a disaster. The boy's mother had promised to come and share the day with him, but the hours slipped away and she never came. Randy hid his tears in the basement, but Snowball found him there. The little dog's tongue worked at washing away the tears, and his tiny nose pushed and nuzzled Randy until he had to laugh. "Forget it all, Randy," Snowball seemed to say, "and let's go play."

Howard Barnes, a veteran of Rainier's psychology department, feels that dogs like Snowball are welcome additions to institutional life. "When things are going wrong, or when your world seems to be falling apart, the dog is there to provide security and love. . . . His presence allows residents to form close personal relationships with a living creature. A love relationship. Sometimes love relationships are hard to find in an institution."

Again, it was virtually by another fortunate accident that Dr. Samuel Corson, a pioneer in the research of dogs used for therapy in hospitals, discovered their effectiveness. He was in the midst of studying behavioral characteristics of various dogs at Ohio State University when complaints started coming in from the staff of a nearby hospital. It seems the dogs' barking was disturbing the hospital's normal peace and quiet. Before Dr. Corson could even consider moving his kennels, it was learned that many of the *patients* at the hospital had a totally different opinion about the barking. Some of them, many of them adolescents who had been withdrawn, broke their silence and asked to be allowed to play with the dogs.

An initial experiment teaming dogs with the patients proved successful, and a nine-month pilot research project, involving fifty psychiatric patients and twenty dogs, was established. Dogs were introduced to the patients in the various wards (occasionally even on the patient's bed) and each patient was allowed to choose which dog he wanted to help groom, walk, and otherwise care for.

Because some patients, at least in the beginning stages of the program, seemed to relate exclusively to the dog, Dr. Corson became concerned that the patients might become attached to their dogs to the permanent exclusion of other people. Such instances, however, did not occur.

Rather, Dr. Corson discovered that many of the patients—some of them originally catatonic—livened up and reached out first to the dogs and eventually to their therapists. "In some cases, the patients' behavior changed almost from the start," the doctor noted. Only two of the fifty patients failed to accept the dogs into their therapy program.

One seventeen-year-old girl, who joined the Corson experiment wholeheartedly, had been hospitalized for several months. "She was schizophrenic pure and simple and had been through all the usual forms of therapy without success," explained the doctor. "She walked like a statue and the only words she said were that she wanted to kill herself."

Then Hal—a young border collie—came into her life. Corson described Hal as an "intelligent, well-mannered dog that responded to orders." Hal's effect on the young woman was astounding, and after a few months of therapy, she received a discharge.

"She's a very beautiful, cheerful and social youngster now," Corson told Ray Freeman of *Dog Fancy* magazine. "She even has talked about becoming a dog trainer."

The nonverbal quality of people-pet relationships is one element that Corson feels is particularly important. "No matter how hard you try when dealing with patients in a psychiatric setting, the signal of pity comes through. . . .

Fox terriers, however, betray no such thing. They'll go up and lick the face of a psychotic patient whose appearance would arouse pity in another human being."

Corson does not believe, however, that every dog or every patient is a candidate for pet therapy. "Dogs must have a diversity of personalities. A reticent dog, for instance, would only strengthen the negative feelings of a patient with paranoia. He might say to himself, 'See, even animals don't like me.'"

Moreover, the doctor emphasizes what has become a litany, that pet therapy is not intended to act as a *substitute* for traditional forms of psychotherapy, but as an *adjunct* to facilitate the resocialization of the patient.

"Resocialization" is, indeed, the goal of the pet-therapy program that has been under way since 1975 at the Lima (Ohio) State Hospital for the Criminally Insane. Housed there are 350 people who have been declared legally insane in court proceedings or who have been unable to cope with serving time in state penitentiaries. The pet program, the brainchild of psychiatric social worker David Lee, started when one of the patients found an injured wild bird and tried to nurse it. "I noticed many of the men got involved with it, and it gave me an idea," Lee recalled recently for writer Patricia Curtis. "I got permission and some money from the superintendent to buy a fish tank and two parakeets as an experiment. Some of the men became very nurturing toward them, and interest spread thrugh the hospital. Then one day, a fellow swiped a parakeet—we found it in his duffle bag. He loved it and couldn't bear to leave it behind."

Lee then decided the patients might benefit from caring for individual pets of their own. "Of course, we don't just turn an animal over to anybody who asks for one—the patients have to earn the right. Each person has to convince us he is ready to take care of an animal."

Lee started his program with two cockatiels, three parakeets, and three aquariums of fish. Growing annually, it now includes more than 160 pets, everything from macaws to gerbils to rabbits and a talkative goose. There are even two deer that live in the hospital courtyard. "One of the deer is so tame, it comes up to search your pockets for treats," reported Miss Curtis. "The other is shy." This second one, "came from a zoo where vandals had stoned it," Lee explained, "and it was not recovering well. The zoo gave the animal to us and the men nursed it back to health . . . but it may never be really friendly."

Happily, there have not been instances of pet abuse among the patients at Lima State. As Patricia Curtis explains, "Nobody would dare harm a pet for fear of retribution from other patients."

The patients' devotion to the pets was apparent one day when a man, trying to avoid taking his medication, threw it into a fifteen-gallon aquarium. Several other patients sprang into action, saved all the fish, and spent the rest of the day cleaning the gravel and resetting the aquarium. Lee believes such experiences only reinforce the patients' feelings of responsibility.

But do the pets really *help* the patients? Lee says yes—the program has produced outstanding results, particularly among patients suffering from depression or suicidal tendencies.

Writer Vicky L. Trussel, profiling Lima State for *American Humane Magazine,* tells of one such patient, a man who had spent four months at the hospital without uttering a word. "The staff introduced him to Gilbert, a female cockatiel. For three weeks the two were inseparable. The bird was kept in a cage by the patient's bed at night and sat perched on his shoulder during the day. The

patient began asking the bird questions, ending his mute-
ness and providing an opportunity for therapy."

Whatever words are used—"providing an opportunity
for therapy" or "initial breakthrough"—this is, of course,
the name of the game, the *raison d'être* for all pet-therapy
programs. Marina Chapman Doyle, writing in *Perspectives
in Psychiatric Care,* speaks of a twelve-week study in which
a single pet rabbit was introduced on a fifteen-bed unit of a
psychiatric hospital. The rabbit, like the pets at Lima State,
served as what some authorities are calling a "social lubri-
cant"—a common departure for communication and
therapeutic activity. "Conversations were increased and
ward meetings were stimulating and active," Doyle says.
"Shared plans, decisions, and projects were initiated as a
result of the rabbit." Even the more regressed patients reportedly appeared to "incorporate its presence into their
personalized reality and thus related to it at a primary
level." Put in less clinical terms, it still means they thought
the rabbit was nice to have around.

Phil Arkow of the Humane Society of the Pikes Peak
Region, Colorado Springs, has similarly discovered that the
animals he takes on visits to psychiatric hospitals provide a
common focus for patients, staff, and visitors to discuss and
share. The author of an excellent manual, *Pet Therapy: A
Study of the Use of Companion Animals in Selected Therapies,* Arkow believes that the pets "are perpetually dependent, noncritical, nonthreatening. They accept patients
with handicaps or disfigurements. For a lot of people, the
pet may be the only thing they're living for."

Chris Roberts writes of a patient named Jed who, in
1949, was admitted to the Castle Nursing Home in Millersburg, Ohio, after suffering apparent brain damage in a
fall. Doctors believed the accident had left him deaf and
mute, and for *over twenty-six years,* he lived there in si-

lence. Then, in 1975, Dr. Corson brought a dog named Whisley to the home. Jed smiled, stroked the animal, turned to Corson and asked, "You brought that dog?"

Such breakthroughs make all the long hours spent by pet therapists worthwhile. Ted Thomas of the Antietam Humane Society (Waynesboro, Pennsylvania), has seen such miracles happen time and time again when he takes shelter animals on visits to the nearby South Mountain Restoration Center, a 740-patient institution. Patients take turns cuddling and hugging the animals. "I'm not sure why it works," Thomas admits, "but it works. Even the quiet ones begin yapping with the dogs."

"I get fantastic feedbacks from the kids," says Nancy Stanley, who takes her Tender Loving Zoo (puppies and kittens) to San Diego's Revere Development Center for handicapped children. "I see special things in their eyes when they play with these pets."

The *Today* show recently celebrated the tenth anniversary of Catharine Kelly's Pet a Pet program in Savannah, Georgia. Every week for over a decade now, Catharine has been taking two or three dogs to the Georgia Regional Hospital for retarded children to see. "These youngsters relate better to animals than to human beings," she says—a statement we have heard over and over from most of the therapists. Miss Kelly recalled one boy who successfully gave obedience commands to one of her dogs. When the dog obeyed, it gave the child an immense feeling of accomplishment.

Kittens, not often used in pet-therapy situations (because of their feline sense of independence) are welcome visitors in the special-education classroom of Melanie Giles, a teacher of emotionally disturbed children in Fairfax, Virginia. Dr. Charles Larson reports in *Cats Magazine* that "Just the sight of the frolicsome felines seems to distract the youngsters from their inner woes, and each child

eagerly rushes to fondle and play with the visiting enter-
tainers. Days after the kittens have returned to their home,
the children continue to benefit from the experience, feeling more positive about themselves and better able to make
contact with others." This, I must add, is where watchful
supervision has to be maintained to make sure the kittens
are not the worse for all the affectionate and enthusiastic
wear.

Dr. Jon Geis found his two cats, Charlie and Gunther,
invaluable in sessions with patients. They served as ice-
breakers, furnishing opening gambits of conversation with
nervous people. The people's reaction to them, or the words
they spoke to them, were often revealing. Most helpful of
all, Dr. Geis said, was using them to illustrate the aspect of
"being." Dr. Geis would say to a patient, "Now, Charlie
here doesn't give a good * * * * about how much value he is to
himself. . . . He just goes ahead and is what he is. He's
more focused on *being* than on being *something*."

Perhaps the most famous feline in the pet-therapy world
is—no, not Morris—Tiger, a mixed-breed cat rescued from
certain death at a Green Bay, Wisconsin, animal shelter by
Sister Jane Tojek, a teacher at St. Joseph's Home for Children. Although the sister was not supposed to have a pet,
she took Tiger back to the home anyway and nursed him
back to health. That was in 1973. Within weeks Tiger became firmly ensconced as a resident "therapist" at the home.

St. Joseph's is a residential center for court-committed
boys, aged seven to eighteen. Some of the youths have
been mistreated or neglected by parents. Others are too
emotionally disturbed to be placed in foster homes. A few
are retarded. Almost all of the boys—whatever their backgrounds—responded to Tiger.

When *American Humane Magazine* interviewed Sister
Jane in 1977, she commented that whenever there is a fight
or altercation at the home, the boy responsible is sent off

by himself with only Tiger for company. "After a few minutes of 'positive strokes' in both directions, the problem usually subsides." Tiger also helps the boys acquire new self-esteem by accepting them just the way they are.

Tiger even helped one small boy work on (if not totally conquer) his fear of animals. Sister Jane encouraged the lad to associate with Tiger as much as possible, and little by little he welcomed the cat's friendship. When he went on a vacation to his home, he missed Tiger so much that he sought a replacement. He confessed to Sister Jane, "I spent three dollars for a cat that looks just like Tiger. And isn't that something? Because I'm still afraid of cats and dogs."

Tiger was one of two felines to be named in 1974 as Top Cats in an annual award given by the Pet Food Institute to dramatize a cat's ability to be a loyal, affectionate companion. The second award winner was Momma Cat, a resident "therapist" at Barboursville State Hospital in Barboursville, West Virginia. Her job is to provide love and friendship for some ninety-eight mentally retarded adults.

"The cat relates to her friends in a way no one of normal IQ can," said Justine Koch, director of volunteer services at the hospital. "Momma Cat is undemanding and cooperative. She responds to the patients on a level they can comprehend and deal with."

Mrs. Koch told of a heart-tugging incident to illustrate the patients' affection for Momma. Each day the patients look forward to their single cups of coffee. One day, shortly after they were served, Mrs. Koch found three cups of coffee placed next to Momma Cat's food dish. "That's how much they love her," she said.

Momma Cat has been entered in many local cat and pet shows, and when she wins, her ribbons provide the patients with great feelings of pride—something long absent from many of their lives.

*   *   *

With the number and variation of pet-therapy efforts continuing to increase, problems are inevitable. In the wave of enthusiasm over the potential benefits inherent in such programs, even the more scientifically inclined lean toward a position of advocacy. There is a tendency to minimize the negative effects through vague, rather than detailed, reports of what *doesn't* work.

We can hope that this situation is now being addressed. Just as valuable as glowing success stories would be systematic collection detailing pet-therapy failures, so that the points of weakness could be identified and avoided in subsequent programs. Good intentions must be supported by adequate and objective research.

Pinpointing what didn't work in certain situations would give a clearer picture of where pet-facilitated treatment would not be advisable at all. A number of problems could be avoided by having some gauge by which each circumstance could be evaluated and the hit-or-miss approach eliminated.

There are several problems that can be assumed to be avoidable if confronted before the fact:

In any pet-therapy effort, a major contributing factor to its success or failure is the attitude of the staff. This is especially true in dealing with the acutely sensitive mentally or emotionally ill. Members of the staff are in the same position of influence over their patients as are parents over children: Their positive or negative approach will be quickly reflected by the individuals in their care.

Plans for setting up guidelines and policies in an animal-facilitated therapy program should include the question of who will be dealing with the situation on the front lines . . . day to day, patient to patient. Some places—those under-staffed, or those where there is a built-in dislike of animals—would do well to address these problems early, to prevent a possible undermining of the program at a later date.

The safety of the patients and the welfare of the animals must both be taken into careful consideration. One way of accomplishing both, which is being used with some success, is maintaining a "pet-therapy room" or "area." In this system, the patients have the privilege of spending time with the pets, either singly or in small groups—and they sometimes have to work to merit this bonus. This keeps the animals in a more controlled situation. It protects those who are not pet-oriented, prevents jealousy and over-possessiveness, and gives the animals a respite from constant interaction with the patients.

A prime requisite in setting up any kind of pet-therapy program must be good judgment and an ability to view the existing situation from *all* perspectives. Failure to do this can result in more harm than good.

We recently heard a story about an elderly dog being introduced as a companion animal for the patients in a psychiatric ward. The dog performed admirably, providing love and affection for all concerned. One patient, habitually suspicious and uncommunicative, opened up as soon as the dog arrived. She took over managing the dog whenever she could. Problems developed, of course, when bad arthritis necessitated the dog's being put to sleep. The woman reverted to her old sullen ways and refused to accept the new dog introduced on the ward.

Allowing too close a relationship between one patient and one dog is dangerous at best. The fact that the dog was elderly to begin with compounded the potential problem even further. In this particular case, it was not too surprising that the patient lost all the benefit of the association and was moved to say, "Oh, yes, I suppose you are just waiting for me to get old and stiff so you can bump me off, aren't you?"

Not all pet-facilitated psychotherapy, of course, happens in schools or hospitals or even in doctors' offices. People have been using pets for years, not knowing the whys or hows, but merely because the little animals make people feel better.

Frances Farmer, a movie star of the 1930's and '40's, has been "rediscovered" of late, thanks primarily to a theatrical motion picture and a made-for-television movie about her life. Miss Farmer spent many years in mental institutions and, once released, suffered periodic lapses into depression and was known to forget her troubles with alcohol. One particularly bad period—one not covered in either movie—occurred in the late 1960's, after Frances had been fired from her job as on-camera hostess of an afternoon movie series on an Indianapolis television station. A friend, looking for a way to help, brought Frances a pet. Miss Farmer described the gift—and its effects—in her autobiography, *Will There Really Be a Morning?*:*

> She brought home a tiny kitten, not more than six weeks old, whose four paws had been nearly burned off. The little creature had obviously been tortured and was unable to walk. She laid it on the bed and said, "I found this, Frances, and I thought maybe you'd know what to do about it."

Frances's first reaction was one of panic—she wanted nothing to do with the kitten. But watching its desperate attempts to fend for itself melted her disdain. "I grumbled and groaned," she recalled, "but finally reached down and stroked its tiny head. It seems it is not uncommon for kittens to be mistreated in such a way, although I could never accept the reality of such horror."

A call was placed to a nearby veterinarian, who prescribed an ointment that needed to be applied to the cat's

* Putnam's, 1972.

paws every three hours, around the clock. Although curs-
ing her friend for having foisted this new responsibility on
her, Frances set about to care for the kitten. She also set
her alarm clock and—knowing she would have to get up
every three hours to apply medicine—she decided to forgo
her usual evening nightcaps.

Frances named her patient Holly-go-lightly, after the
Truman Capote character, and placed it at the foot of her
own bed. "But it would wiggle itself up," she remembered
later, "and despite the fact that it couldn't walk, it would
somehow end up on my pillow . . . and I left it there beside me."

Outwardly still grumbling that once Holly's paws had
healed, out she'd go, Frances secretly loved having a new
purpose in life. Holly was soon joined by Clarence, another
stray kitten who had been severely wounded in a neighborhood dogfight. Then Holly got "in the family way," and
Frances had to help care for six newborns. Finally, yet another feline was found, this one hobbling as though one leg
had been cut off. The veterinarian diagnosed that the poor
creature had probably been hit by a car—its leg was not
broken but shoved up into the shoulder socket. Once
again, Nurse Farmer answered the call to duty. Soon word
of Frances's kittens got out, and friends (and their families)
were stopping by to visit.

Frances summed up the whole experience in her book:

And there I was, a hard-bitten old dame, caught
in the middle with kids running in and out, people
dropping in, unannounced, and cats peeking at me
from every corner. What had once been a dry
crusty house was suddenly coming alive. . . .
There had been a gradual awakening within me, a
strange and exciting stirring of self-dignity, almost
like a rebirth. . . . There was a new complexion to

my life. . . . I was striding into a marvelous and unique universe.

The number of individual case histories, individual pet-therapy programs, as you can see, is burgeoning. Each of the programs has started tentatively and, with experience, has come to the awareness of strengths and weaknesses. But in each case, *something* has been learned that will eventually build a clear pattern to follow.

Dr. Michael McCulloch put it all into perspective when he said, "All of us who are concerned about the health and well-being of living things must never abandon those whom we cannot cure. We must continue to help patients maintain hope and the will to survive. To those suffering disability, self-esteem and dignity are essential. Our efforts to care and to comfort in their moments of deep despair must never stop. *'Cure when possible, but comfort always.'*"

8.

Pets for Institutions

Perhaps the most startling changes being brought about by the current surge of interest in the human/animal bond is the introduction of animals as therapists in such once-stolid institutions as hospitals and prisons.

Indeed, because animals have been found to provide physiological as well as psychological benefits to human health, a few medical hospitals around the country have initiated full pet-therapy programs or, at least, have softened their long-standing rules against having animals on the premises.

My first experience with this phenomenon occurred a couple of years ago, while Allen was hospitalized at a major Los Angeles hospital. We had been aware of a patient down the hall who was depressed and not responding well to medication, and those dear nurses kept fretting. His doctor finally discovered that the man was worried about his little dog at home, who, in turn, was so forlorn without his master that he was refusing to touch his food. The hospital staff agreed to allow something quite unorthodox for this antiseptic environment—they agreed to allow the man's dog to be brought into the hospital, onto the floor, into the man's room every day at feeding time. The dog, excited about being reunited with his master, began eating again.

The man, relieved that his pet was eating, relaxed and let the medication go to work. Within a few weeks, the fellow had improved sufficiently to be sent home.

A small dog is one thing to bring into a hospital setting rather unobtrusively; however, it seems where there's a will, no challenge is too great to find a way. A fourteen-year-old girl, Claire, had an all-consuming interest in horses and ponies. When it was discovered that her condition was terminal cancer, she filled the long inactive days studying and writing about them. Eventually, she went to the hospital for the last time, and I will quote the story as it was told by Keith Webb of the Diamond Riding Centre:

"During her brief periods of consciousness, the telephone would ring at the Centre and her favorite pony would set out for the ward. He would put his head through the open window for her to see him. The contrast between the clinical atmosphere of the ward, and that of a shaggy, smelly pony was quite dramatic." Cards . . . pictures . . . models . . . ornaments. When Claire died, her room was full of ponies.

Research is under way investigating the real possibility that pet ownership can actually extend human life. Dr. Aaron Katcher and Dr. Erika Friedmann, for example, studied ninety-two patients who had been hospitalized for coronary problems. Of the fifty-three patients who had pets, only three died; but of the thirty-nine patients without pets, eleven died within a year. Formal studies of patients associating with pets within the hospital settings, however, are, sadly, still missing. Margaret Noctor, R.N., who co-authored the Katcher-Friedmann study, feels that inside or outside the hospital, pets seem to give patients "someone else to live for. The pet cannot survive without its owner, and they feel needed."

Dr. Bustad highly recommends that hospital admission

forms include the questions: Do you live alone? Do you have a pet or pets at home? He also advocates wallet cards alerting that there are pets at home in the event of an accident. Both of these small considerations could do much to alleviate unnecessary anxiety on the part of the patient.

Dr. Friedmann advises that heart patients not be counseled to give up their pets when they enter the hospital, a practice that has often happened in the past. Rather, the patients should be questioned about making arrangements for the care of the pets during their stay.

Some patients are becoming more and more adamant about taking their pets along to the hospitals. United Press International recently ran a story about such a case. "Arthur McDougall, 88, hugs his French poodle, 15, after both were admitted to Salinas convalescent hospital. McDougall refused to enter the hospital without the dog, who is deaf and partially blind, so the hospital agreed to admit the pooch."

There are those, of course, who are unable to look ahead for very long. For them, the comfort becomes even more important. In Glasgow, Scotland, Dr. Bustad tells of hospices using specially selected cats for those who are terminally ill. Some cats adapt readily . . . lying quietly next to the patient and lessening the fear of dying alone.

Closer to home, a dear friend of ours was comforted in just such a way. Prettypuss stayed with Lenore through all the last weeks. During the last few days, she would only leave Lenore's side momentarily, then rush back and touch her mistress's face lightly with a soft paw. "I'm back."

Admittedly, there is a difference between a convalescent hospital and a regular health-care facility, but the success of pet-therapy programs in the former is being noticed by interested staff in the latter.

Golden West Convalescent Home in Hawthorne, California, houses some ninety-nine patients aged twenty-nine to one hundred two. It recently adopted an eight-month-old mixed-breed therapist named Dutchess . . . who took to her new job like a duck to water.

"We were flabbergasted," said administrator Marion Hames. "Without any training or coaxing on our part, she visits each of our forty rooms by herself every day and makes rounds at night. If a patient's light goes on, Dutchess will head right for the room and wait until the nurse comes. We lock the main door at night, and if anybody shows up, the dog will growl and bark, which is the only time she does that."

Hames indicates Dutchess has had a great calming effect on all the patients. One woman in particular, a twenty-nine-year-old patient dying from multiple sclerosis, became depressed and hysterical one day. The nurses and orderlies were not able to calm her down . . . but Dutchess was. "Dutchess came and put her head on the patient's knee. The girl relaxed and began to scratch behind the dog's ears. Then she let a nurse help her back to bed.

"One man had been suicidal. He had been brought here after hitting himself repeatedly on the head with a hammer. He doesn't speak English, but dog language is universal. Since Dutchess's arrival, the man smiles, holds out his hand for her, and our psychiatrist has detected a definite change in outlook. He is much more relaxed."

The most famous resident four-legged therapist in any hospital environment is, undoubtedly, Skeezer. *The Dog That Healed* was the book that told her life story, later made into a movie for television. For seven years Skeezer was on duty at the Children's Psychiatric Hospital, part of the University of Michigan Medical Center in Ann Arbor. A stray, of uncertain lineage, she was brought in as an "experimental therapeutic device," at the suggestion of the doctors at CPH. Small animals—gerbils, hamsters, fish, and birds—had been used as diversions from time to time, but while the children found them fascinating at first, it was difficult to relate to them.

When a dog was suggested, there were some objections involving behavior and sanitation, but these were overruled and the Animal Research Laboratory at the university was asked to supply a puppy. And a playful puppy she was, with growing up of her own to do. Alice Williams, the nurse in charge of the sixth floor, took Skeezer home with her for a few days of intensive training. Through the next months, the dog would run in the hall with the children, tumble in play, then fall suddenly asleep, puppy fashion, on a bed or under a nurse's desk. She made mistakes, was rebuked, but learned fast, and by the time she was a year old Skeezer had the job nailed down. Instinctively, she seemed to know who needed comforting, or play, or perhaps just a willing ear. "Leave it to Skeezer" became a byword on the ward.

At eighteen months, Skeezer became a mother—by her Siberian husky friend belonging to a medical student who would come to visit the ward—and her nine puppies were a delightful learning experience for the children. When homes were found for all, Skeezer was spayed and settled down to the serious business of being a nurse.

After seven years there was a change in direction of the children's psychiatric program, and Skeezer was retired. She went to live with her good friend and "boss," Alice Williams, at her home in Wisconsin. Alice Williams feels that "Skeezer proved that with proper training a dog can help open pathways into the minds and hearts of disturbed children. I hope her example will inspire others to start similar programs of therapy."

Geraldine Ross, writing in *National Humane Review*, indicates that none of this is really "new." She tells of the therapeutic effect a little pet turtle named Chum had on

her and other residents in a convalescent home for tuber-
culosis patients back in the early 1940's. Larger pets were
not allowed, but this little guy became the center of conversation and attention among all the patients.

Some hospitals today, particularly pediatric facilities,
allow pet visitation programs. One large teaching hospital
here in Los Angeles allows dogs to visit children who are
frightened, perhaps away from home for the first time,
often awaiting an operation. Writer Helen Whitaker explains that these dogs "listen to long stories that doctors
and nurses don't have time for, but that children need to
tell. They are also something to hold on to and pat until
finally a frightened hand relaxes and the child sleeps."

Twice a week, docents from the Los Angeles Zoo
bring animals to the Children's Hospital—various birds,
rabbits, reptiles. (Harvey, the snake, is a regular member
of the group.) The children are not allowed to touch the
animals, but they look forward to the visit because it allows
them to forget their maladies, at least for a while.

The visitors are permitted into certain areas where
they have free rein—the rehabilitation section, the dialysis
and laminar-flow areas, and the sixth floor. First they put
on a slide program, then the women proceed to the sixth
floor where they go from room to room with their animals.
Ruth Joyce, a docent, has been making these visits for over
five years. She recalled for me recently one incident when
she was making the rounds of the sixth floor carrying a lop-
eared rabbit. When she entered one young patient's room,
the boy looked up and started talking lickity-split in Spanish. Sensing something might not be quite right, Ruth
backed out of the room and continued on her rounds. A
few minutes later, a rather animated doctor caught up with
her. "Do you know what you've done?" he demanded.
Ruth cringed . . . expecting the worst. "You've gotten that

boy to open up! He hasn't said one word in all the days he's been here . . . to anyone . . . until you walked in with your rabbit!"

Ruth tells of another little girl, about three years old. She had been brought on a gurney to see the visitor that particular day, a two-year-old chimpanzee. The little girl began to cry because she couldn't hear. The chimp signed to her . . . needless to say they became fast friends.

Children's Memorial Hospital in Chicago allows volunteers from the Anti-Cruelty Society to bring in a batch of puppies two or three times a month for a petting and hugging session. "When we first got permission to bring pets here," reported volunteer Ginny Anderson, "some of the doctors and nurses disapproved. They envisioned mess, noise, germs, all sorts of problems. Now, they welcome us because the pets do the kids so much good."

Reporting the phenomenon on the television series *60 Minutes,* Harry Reasoner added, "At this hospital, doctors and nurses have found that many of the children cooperate better with the treatment and therapy after the puppy visits."

Patricia Curtis, preparing an article in 1981 for *Smithsonian* magazine, visited the hospital and reported the love-in she found:

Even though many of the children are very sick or badly injured, almost all are eager to hold the pets. A beautiful child in pigtails sees us in the hall and her eyes grow wide. Her mother props her up. The little girl cannot speak and lacks motor control of her arms, but she manages to draw Miss Anderson's hand close to her face so she can nuzzle a kitten.

A quadriplegic boy of about twelve is asked if

he would like to see a dog. "Yep," he whispers. The pup's warm body is held against the boy's cheek. He smiles.

A wisp of a child attached to bottles and machines lies in her mother's lap in another room. Quietly we ask the mother if the child would like to pet a kitten. We are abashed in the presence of so much pain. But the child smiles, raises her hand to run it over the kitten . . .

The Johnston R. Bowman Health Center for the Elderly, also in Chicago, has found that such visits of animals from the Anti-Cruelty Society have been very beneficial in meeting many of the psychosocial needs of their elderly patients. Ellen M. Jessee, supervisor of recreation therapy for the center, says that the puppies and kittens that are brought in each week serve as catalysts for reaching individuals who are isolated or withdrawn. "This program contributes to a supportive, homelike environment at J.R.B. that promotes independence and enables many individuals to achieve their maximum level of functioning and return to the community."

Some hospitals and staffs have an understandable reluctance to allow pets onto the wards, even though great care is taken to avoid areas where there might be special vulnerability. As Dr. Gloria Francis, professor and director of research for the School of Nursing, Virginia Commonwealth University, explains, "The transition from a sterile, sober and sedate ward to a near normal, homelike environment with a dog or two is a *radical change* [italics added]." She cites a study by C. M. Brickel, in which a group of cats was added to a hospital ward and enhanced total-care patients' level of responsiveness to the entire ward environment. She cautions that the anticipation of short-term problems should not prevent nurses from imagining the positive long-range impact of pet therapy.

Dr. Francis concludes: "Pet therapy may well be a major part of residential health care facilities' psychotherapeutic programs in the future. . . . Animals' role in human companionship, pleasure and comfort is now being understood also as a healing one. The evidence is clear; opportunities are present. It is up to nursing to be informed, open, and willing to explore a potentially therapeutic resource . . . an animal friend."

Prisons and other correctional facilities, like hospitals, have long been devoid of any of the trappings of a homelike atmosphere . . . but, as with hospitals, this situation is changing.

Ironically, perhaps the most celebrated case in the history of pet-facilitated therapy occurred in a prison . . . the case of Robert Stroud, the famous "Birdman of Alcatraz."

Most of us are aware that there was such a man. . . . Burt Lancaster portrayed him in the movie made from Thomas Gaddis's book, *Birdman of Alcatraz*. Beyond that, perhaps, the details have been blurred by time. It came as a surprise to me to realize that Stroud's association with his birds began as far back as 1920, when he found his first fallen nest of baby sparrows in the prison yard. Two of the nestlings survived, and his patience was rewarded when they learned to obey his commands . . . to come to him, fly to his bunk, roll over and play dead . . . all at the snap of a finger. His interest expanded from entertainment to serious study. The sparrows were joined by canaries . . . and by 1930, Robert Stroud found that he had become an international authority. No one was aware that he was in prison. To this day, his book, *Stroud's Digest of the Diseases of Birds,* is in every library and is still considered somewhat of an avian bible, worldwide.

Robert Stroud's fascination with birds spread to some of the other prisoners in the same isolation wing, and even to some of the guards in charge. The story of Stroud's life is certainly not a happy one, but his passion for the study of birds furnished a source of nonprison communication with everyone with whom he came in contact, and a link with the world outside.

Phil Arkow, of the Humane Society of the Pikes Peak Area, says, "Since that time, a small but growing number of correctional institutions have allowed, and encouraged, their inmates to enjoy the companionship, the purpose, and the responsibility that pets can provide."

We have already introduced you to David Lee's pet-therapy program at the Lima (Ohio) State Hospital for the Criminally Insane. It is one of the most successful efforts of its type, and also has one of the longest track records. This institutional therapeutic pet program has continued without interruption since 1973. It has even balanced its annual expenses for animal care and feeding by selling animal offspring, and by other fund raisers through the year. They even have their own "humane society" set up on the inside.

Inmates care for the community animals in the courtyard to earn the right to a pet of their own to care for. These animals are the only things that belong to them; it is that responsibility that leads to necessary communication with staff members, and results in more interaction with fellow inmates.

The success stories are legion—and sometimes dramatic. In relating how tensions have eased between the men on the ward since the animals came on the scene, the story is told of one of the men who went berserk. In his fury, he broke all the furniture in the day room . . . but he left the cage of birds intact! Therapists found an advantage in talking to an inmate on the other side of a fish tank, since it allowed them to establish eye contact through the tank during the discussion . . . not always easy under other circumstances. It made inmates accessible to treatment.

David Lee explained that one of the major problems they face is establishing communication: "These people are social outcasts and usually see no reason to talk to or trust staff members. Giving pets to the patients is a way of showing that we were human, that we cared about them, and were willing to put a degree of trust in them. It was a way of saying that we thought they could handle the responsibility of caring for a living creature."

Another interesting, yet totally different, prison program is in operation at Purdy Women's Prison in Tacoma, Washington, under the direction of Kathy Quinn.

Working with Washington State University, Tacoma Community College, and the Department of Corrections, Kathy has developed a program, using dogs, which enables volunteer inmates to improve themselves, and at the same time be of help to those on the outside. The project, called Help 'N' Hands, in Kathy's words, "teaches volunteer inmates how to train dogs to help the elderly and many kinds of handicapped persons. The prisoners benefit from learning the vocation of dog training, and the elderly and handicapped benefit from receiving well-trained canine helpmates."

In the program, established in October 1982, inmates also learn to groom and give obedience training (for a fee) to dogs owned by the general public. The prison views this idea favorably for many reasons: It not only improves morale, but it provides vocational training for the women to use when they get out of prison. Perhaps the clincher is that by charging the public for the obedience training it makes the program cost-effective.

At Purdy Treatment Center for Women this pilot undertaking is making Pacific Northwest prison history. Up to seventeen inmates may participate in the program at a time. Some of the women at the prison, of course, are afraid of animals, and their wish to stay away from the dogs is respected. Because the classes—lectures and hands-on training—are conducted on the premises, in the prison gymnasium and ballfield, every precaution is taken to keep these areas clean. A subject of considerable concern is fleas. The grounds as well as the dogs are given a good dousing of flea spray after every training session. Kathy is all too aware of what occurred in 1976 at San Quentin (California) State Prison. . . .

For a few years prior to 1976, stray cats were allowed (unofficially) to be kept as pets and mascots by inmates at San Quentin. The practice was tolerated by officials, who realized that the cats helped some prisoners maintain a better state of morale. However, as the number of cats continued to increase, no provision was made against fleas, lice, and simply the odor created by so many felines. The non-pet owners had valid complaints, and the cats were ultimately banished from the prison. This was a classic example of wrong planning . . . or worse, no planning at all.

Kathy and her staff work overtime to be sure a similar situation never occurs at Purdy.

The dogs used in the Purdy program are brought in from a local kennel for each training session. Soon, however, construction will be completed on a new on-site kennel, complete with runs for up to ten large dogs.

Guests from the outside are an exciting by-product of the pet program. Those who will be the handicapped recipients of the dogs-in-training, for example, visit the inmate-trainees, generating in the prisoners a renewed sense of purpose. Various "observers" are also welcomed. An AKC judge was recently invited to observe the first prisonwide dog show. Such events, and the favorable publicity they generate, help build needed self-esteem in the prisoners, who, as Kathy says, "suddenly have reason to think, 'Hey, maybe I'm not so bad after all.'"

The prisoners involved in the first year of the Prison Pet Partnership Program were recently asked to evaluate themselves and their experience. Following are a few of their comments:

> This program is the most positive influence I've had in the past five years. It has enabled me to realize things about myself, and has taught me many new skills. Having access to these dogs twice a week has helped me realize too that I am still capable of responding to living creatures and has put me in touch with feelings I was sure I had lost. I'd like to be around the dogs five days a week, I enjoy it so much. . . .

> I am thoroughly enjoying the program. I am able to maintain a happy positive state of mind when I'm here with my fine "furry friends." It takes my mind off the fact that I am incarcerated. I'm looking forward to the kennels being built so possibly I could have a dog of my own to train. I have a favorite puppy that I love very much, and her name is Lacy. She makes me feel good and helps take my loneliness away, because she's so lovable. . . .

> I think this canine program is great! Not only has it taught me about dogs, it showed me a different side to some inmates I generally wouldn't deal with. . . .

> I am proud to be a part of this program. It gives me a good feeling to know that we are all helping some person on the outside by training these dogs. . . .

My sister raises Dobermans and now that I've learned something about dogs, I'll be able to help train hers. Which would be a better experience for me, so I'll be able to get a job in working with dogs. . . .

This program is the nicest and most pleasant experience. I find working with Glory, I don't keep so much inside, but talk to her. I know she'll be gone one of these days real soon, and we'll all need a box of Kleenex, but she'll be so good for Burt. Working and training these dogs does something good inside, and knowing that in some way these dogs will help another in need. I'm doing life, and hope this program will be here for a long, long time. . . .

The class is great! The instructors are dynamite! The response from students is outstanding! We are learning so much. From all the knowledge, people involved with animals (that come to our class)—vets, trainers, techs, etc.—and proper instruction, I have decided to remain in the field. My biggest plan is to utilize my knowledge and interest to reach poverty-stricken street kids in the ghetto of Seattle, and hopefully change their life around. I want to mold bad and undisciplined kids to useful citizens. I plan to get them involved with dogs. To help them make dog training a useful and enjoyable hobby. But most of all, something positive to do and seeing that the animal is a creation from God. I love the class. It has brought a positive change in my life. It is working!

Kathy Quinn, who credits her animal friends with building her own self-esteem, seems uniquely qualified to spearhead a prison pet-partnership program. The inmates respect her, not only because her love for animals is so apparent, but because she had had a skirmish or two with the Establishment herself. She is a good role model for each of them . . . now.

After running away from home at age sixteen, Kathy was locked up thirty-six different times in fourteen mental institutions for a total of seven years. Recalling those times today, she says, "I was labeled 'retarded' mostly because of my behavior. I was so self-destructive, this was the best way they could control me . . . hog-tied in a straitjacket."

When she was finally released, Kathy had major problems associating and communicating with people. She didn't know how. She spent her days inside, in her apartment, then went for long walks alone after dark. Seldom were words spoken to anybody.

Extremely lonely, Kathy remembered Bonnie, a dog she'd had as a child. She decided to adopt a new dog and wrote to various kennels seeking assistance. A kennel in Texas offered to give her a German shepherd . . . for the cost of shipping. Kathy didn't have the funds, but a couple of policewomen who had befriended her quickly came up with the coin.

Kathy named her new friend Jony, and together they "took off" roaming the countryside. Interestingly, now when the police stopped her, "they didn't just drag me away," she recalls. "Rather they tried to get me to talk, first about Jony, then about myself."

Jony was soon joined by three more German shepherds. "The more dogs I had, the more people wanted to know about them. The dogs made me control my life. My self-destructive behavior ceased."

Evaluating the situation now, Kathy admits that she selected pure-bred German shepherds out of vanity, out of the need for an ego boost. She wanted her dogs to be something she felt she herself was not—beautiful and worthy of attention. A mixed-breed pound dog, however loving, would not at this time have done as much for her self-image.

The size of the German shepherds, of course, also gave her a certain sense of security. But, as she admits, "It was very hard to live on welfare with four big dogs," so, as soon as she felt able, she gave them away. "The better I got with my life, the less I needed the big dogs."

She did still need companionship, however, and soon adopted a couple of "lap-size" dogs: Billy, a white terrier mix, and Andy, a Yorkshire, both of whom she promptly trained. Not only did these dogs help Kathy get over the rest of her shyness, she returned the favor with little Andy. Originally terrified of strangers, Andy trusted only Kathy and Billy (who hadn't a lick of shyness in his whole body). Kathy tuned in very quickly to the problem, then found a clever way to solve it. Remembering how she herself had once felt when meeting strangers in the company of Jony, she decided Andy would feel less threatened if he met strangers in the company of his own "canine companion," Billy. She would take the dogs for a walk, and when anyone expressed interest in petting them, she'd put Andy's leash in Billy's mouth, and tell them to approach the person. Andy, trusting Billy implicitly, went along, however timidly, and soon discovered there was nothing to fear.

Today, Kathy works similar magic with the inmates. Among her volunteers are some hard-core types; three are serving long terms for homicide. Most are young mothers with children, looking toward a new future when they get out. All respond to the animals who don't make judgments.

Kathy says, "I feel that people coming out of institutions are having a hard time. They're released and they can't function. Everything they are used to doing is in chaos. This is a great time for them to have an animal. Our training program helps people become responsible with themselves. It gives them something to do . . . a skill . . . and that, in turn, builds their self-confidence."

Kathy's own self-confidence has never been higher. Thanks to her work with animals, she is now not only working with the Purdy prison program, she's an accomplished animal photographer, the writer of magazine articles, and . . . a public speaker! She gave a talk in 1979 at the national meeting on Pet Facilitated Therapy in California; she gave a two-day workshop on dogs trained for the disabled at the American Humane Association Convention in Denver in 1980; and in October 1981, she presented a workshop at the prestigious International Conference on the Human/Companion Animal Bond in Philadelphia. Not bad for a girl who was once too reticent to speak her own name.

Kathy works closely with Dr. Leo Bustad and Linda Hines in their People Pet Partnership at Washington State University. Linda says of Kathy's Help 'N' Hands, "Want help? Why not get a Purdy dog." Kathy's success is truly inspiring.

The District of Columbia Department of Corrections central prison facility in Lorton, Virginia, has a pet therapy program of its own entitled P.A.L.—People-Animals-Love. Under the supervision of Dr. Earl O. Strimple, each of forty inmates has an animal for which he is personally responsible. Included in the menagerie are fish, birds, guinea pigs, cats, and rabbits.

The purpose of the program, as defined by its bylaws, is "to set forth the concept of companionship and to deliver to the residents . . . a revitalized and effective challenge in love and sharing of humanity."

According to Dr. Strimple, "People need to love and be loved, need to feel needed, need to feel worthwhile, need responsibility. Animals do provide noncritical and nonjudgmental love. They accept you as you are. These animals may help the residents to distinguish their own problems and the realities on the outside."

Again, the prisoners actually participating in the P.A.L. program were asked how *they* felt about it.

It gives a new direction of thought and a new and positive involvement.

It will allow me to develop patience and also allow me to utilize my free time more wisely.

It will give the participant a responsibility and will take their minds off hurting others.

They are warm and friendly and seem to understand.

In confinement you can't show love to anyone, and I don't want to become hard.

And, as one inmate explained, "You know what animals have got that some men haven't? Plain common sense. That's what dogs and birds will teach you if you don't watch out."

Similarly, the California Institution for Women at Frontera allowed prisoners to have birds as personal pets in their cells. Unfortunately, overcrowding is taking its toll, and they are having to double up. As it now stands, those who already have pet birds can keep them, but no new ones can be added. As prisoners are released they take their pets with them, so it is a gradual phaseout—not, however, because the practice failed.

Dart Anthony, chairman of the Las Vegas Humane Society, reports an effort is under way to establish a pet-therapy project in Nevada state prisons. Because the state has a huge population of wild horses and burros, Anthony's plans include a program in which inmates could "hire out" to work with these wild animals and, in so doing, gain a marketable job skill.

All these programs are noteworthy, and the results from the inside have been gratifying. Do they really help when a prisoner is released?

There are already many rehabilitation centers, halfway houses, etc., around the country providing opportunities for the people with animal-related skills. Pat Prescott, director of the Delaware Humane Association, for example, hires carefully selected juvenile delinquents who are on probation or just out of prison, and has them work in the shelter. She has "employed" approximately forty such youths since the program started in 1978, all of them between the ages of thirteen and sixteen.

Pat told us recently that she's witnessed remarkable changes in these teenagers as they've put in their hours at the shelter. One lad came in two years ago, totally down on the world. He learned to relax and come to terms with himself . . . and the world . . . while at the shelter, has since gone back to finish high school, and has plans to proceed with college.

One girl, a fifteen-year-old currently in the program, enjoys the animals so much she hates to go home at the end of a day. She puts in far and away more hours per week than required. Her interest in the animals has spurred her interest in other areas that, before this, held no meaning. Pat is currently teaching the girl elementary mathematics (addition and subtraction), for example.

There is an assortment of animals housed in the shelter—including cats, dogs, deer, skunks, guinea pigs, turtles, even baby squirrels. The youths learn to clean and care for the animals, and because the shelter is open to the general public, they also learn to dress themselves properly, keep themselves presentable, and speak politely with the visitors. Pat calls her program an "all-around education." It is true that one or two of her graduates have backslid and gotten into trouble again, but the overwhelming majority have gone on to lead happy productive lives.

A similar project was started ten years ago in Riverside, California—a youth-activities program that diverts first-time juvenile offenders from the justice system into community-based alternative treatment programs. One such program, like Pat Prescott's, centers on the local Humane Society animal shelter. William Bellamy, executive director of the society when the program was founded, explained, "Because most of these young people had seldom participated in anything where they could succeed, our program was designed so they could not fail. Also, they seldom had experienced anyone showing an interest in themselves as individuals. For the most part, these youngsters have never been able to try something they thought worthwhile without being told 'no.' Each participant in our program experiences doing something in a positive manner with built-in success. It is our hope that this experience will change the youngsters' attitudes about animals, the humane society, and fellow humans."

The Green Chimneys Farm in Brewster, New York, which we mentioned in Chapter Six, has expanded with a new (since 1981) "Project We Serve" program aimed at training Putnam County youth on probation to be aides with the farm's handicapped residents. As executive director Samuel Ross explains it, "We introduce them to career opportunities with plants and animals, and provide them with firsthand experiences with therapeutic riding and farm chores."

A totally different approach is taken by a company in

Tucson, Arizona, called VisionQuest. Theirs is an action-oriented rehabilitation program designed as an alternative for delinquents who would otherwise be facing a sentence to reform school. One part of this program is a wagon train trip—2,500 rough miles with horses, from Tucson to Denver and back. Their mental and physical stamina is put to the daily test, and caring for the horses, it seems, has helped many to relate to other human beings.

Ahead With Horses in Sun Valley, California, Liz Helms's organization also makes use of court-referred volunteers, people who are required to do community service. Liz tells me that these referrals often arrive with something of a chip on their shoulders. They think they've seen it all, and they really don't want to be doing this anyway. Then they spot the children, the handicapped kids who are doing all they can just to survive. The young toughs' hearts usually melt very quickly, and interaction is swift. The disabled children treat these volunteers like gods—which is a boost to anyone's ego. Within days, the volunteers are arriving early and staying late, doing all they can to help. They feel needed, which is something most of them haven't felt before. Even long-established behavior patterns change. Many children are allergic to the grease and sugars of junk food, so the volunteers forgo bringing any with them. Many of the youngsters have trouble breathing, so cigarettes, too, become forgotten. Lastly, being around the children themselves—who are trying *so* hard with *so* little to accomplish *so* much—many delinquents have to totally reevaluate their own priorities. Maybe their lives haven't been so bad after all. They also come in contact with forgiveness. . . .

Everyone knows how important the horses are to the program . . . they bear a great deal of responsibility. If, however, one of the animals makes a mistake, or goes lame, or cannot function one day, no one stops loving it; no one wants to lock it away or punish it. Such forgiveness is often something new for the delinquents who, prior to this, had never received a second chance from others . . . or, most of all, extended one . . . even to themselves.

It seems significant, in light of all these different programs, plus the many more we have not touched upon, that statistics show most parents who abuse children have no history of pet ownership.

On the other side of the world, prisoners and animals are working together in yet a different way. In Australia, there is an established system whereby prisoners are given the responsibility of socializing dogs who will later be used to guide the blind. The puppies stay with the prisoners for fourteen months before being returned for their formal training. The results have proven most successful, with far fewer flunk-outs.

Pet-related rehabilitation programs are also being used in various alcoholic and drug-abuse treatment centers. The Guenster House in Bridgeport, Connecticut, a halfway house for alcoholics, for example, assigns each new guest a puppy. Roger Caras, in his book *A Celebration of Dogs,* writes, "I visited the institution and found that one of the keys to its program of rehabilitation was the dog, specifically the Labrador Retriever. One patient-inmate of twenty-five sat cross-legged on his bed patting his Lab. He sobbed as he confessed to me he had been a skid row bum since the age of sixteen. 'This,' he said, nodding toward his dog, 'is the first responsibility I have ever accepted without panicking.'"

Phil Arkow reports a nursing home in Colorado Springs adopted a dog specifically for an alcoholic patient, and achieved great success. "The dog, Buffy, gave the patient a new interest in life, arrested his drinking problem, and caused the patient to display more interest in group activities."

A friend of mine, a famous actress whom I shall call Alice, who has now been dry for several years, makes no bones about the fact that one of the main influences that pushed her into taking treatment for alcohol was her dog. Alice's friends all worried and did what they could. The problem was she didn't believe she had a problem. It was her dog—her constant companion—who finally got through to her. The dog simply refused to have anything to do with her, or even stay in the same room, when she'd had too much. The message worked!

The recent intense interest in the human/animal bond by the media (especially, but not limited to, the interest in the new use of pets in institutions) invites some predictable problems that could work against the whole concept if not carefully monitored. Many well-meaning individuals, hearing of the therapeutic influence an animal may bring, for example, to an institutional environment, may want to run out, rescue any appealing dog from the nearest shelter, and put him into whatever facility is handy as the new dog-in-residence. Should work wonders for everyone concerned, right? Wrong! That is comparable to Russian roulette. The dogs or cats chosen for such important work must be carefully evaluated as to temperament, health, tolerance, and training. That cannot be stressed enough. The facility involved must be checked out as to where the animal can and cannot be; the patients must be polled to be sure no one will be unduly upset by the advent of a pet, and last, but of equal importance, the staff must be thoroughly dealt in *before* the fact. As we have seen, not doing this can result in the collapse of the whole endeavor. It can also lead to neglect . . . possibly even abuse of the animal itself.

Pet therapy is not a simple procedure—very few worthwhile things are—but with common sense and pre-planning, it can be a most rewarding one.

• Part Three •

Other Aspects of the Bond

"What kind of time they live in
only they know.
On plains, perhaps, in jungle
wilderness, or where bush and thorn
nourish the wildbeast and doe . . ."

—JEAN BURDEN

9.

Our Wild-Animal Bond

We have been addressing people/pet relationships to this point, but in the overall sense of the human/animal bond, we cannot ignore the large part that wild animals play.

For many people, watching wild animals in close proximity stirs something so deep inside that it is hard to identify. It is not entirely unrelated to the therapeutic effect of watching tropical fish to ease stress. Paul Shepard, in his book *Thinking Animals,* said,

> Human evolutionary history grew in the presence of wild creatures. Without such experience, it appears that intellectual and emotional maturity cannot be fully achieved, especially by modern people . . . in urban technological civilizations.

The inner response to this experience goes a long way back in time.

To see these animals running free in their own environment is, of course, the ideal; but for many of them, the encroachment of the human population has all but obliterated their original habitat. The tropical rain forests are shrinking daily as man moves in, displacing spectacular bird and animal life. The image of Africa's unending hordes of wildlife covering the plains is changing as we speak. Even the mighty elephant is threatened; his range covers less and less open territory, leading to shortages of food and water, and a general imbalance in the number of these huge animals in a given space.

Today, of course, we are able to see the animals of the world in their natural habitat without ever having to leave our living room, thanks to the magic of the TV tube. Through countless documentaries there is hardly a creature from any corner of the world, on land, in the air, or under the sea, that has not been brought home to us.

What the documentaries cannot deliver is the experience of seeing these exotic creatures in real, living, breathing, warm-blooded life. So it is not too surprising that attendance at the zoo keeps rising as our appetite for animal knowledge is whetted. Today, more people go to zoos than attend all the sporting events *combined.*

I have been a zoo-phile all my life. As a child, whenever my father would go to San Diego on business, my mother and I would tag along and spend two full days at the San Diego Zoo . . . from early morning until they threw us out at closing time. More often than not, Dad would rush to finish early so he could join us there in the late afternoon. Today, I am serving my tenth year on the board of trustees of the Greater Los Angeles Zoo Association—GLAZA. It isn't quite the Zookeeper that I used to dream of being, but it means I have my very own key to the zoo!

Others must share such a lifelong enthusiasm, since there are more than a few cases of millionaires working as zoo attendants, despite their wealth. At LA Zoo, we have a woman who is a Ph.D. working as a volunteer raking hay and wielding a shovel with the rest.

The first time I went to a zoo with Allen was in St. Louis, Missouri, in 1963. We had been married only about a month, when I went there to do *The King and I* at the Muni Opera. Allen flew out to see opening night, and to spend a few days with me.

With performances in the evening, our days were free, and like any new bride, I expressed a burning desire to visit the St. Louis Zoo. I meant just *go* to the zoo, but Allen had a better idea. Marlin Perkins was director of that fine zoo, and I had been a big follower of his *Zoo Parade* series on television, so . . . Allen called Marlin and explained, "Betty wants to see your zoo. My wife is a little strange!" Marlin replied, "So is mine. Come on over!"

We arrived at the zoo promptly at ten the next morning, and Marlin had arranged for his wife to meet us for a personally conducted tour. I cherish that moment to this day, as it was the first time I laid eyes on a woman who was to become a great and good friend as well as a kindred soul.

Allen used to love to tell this story, and I guess he told it much the way it happened: "We said hello to this pretty lady, I got in the back of the Jeep, so Betty could sit next to Carol, who was driving . . . and that is the last intelligible thing I can remember. These two started talking animals, both *so* excited and fighting for words, and to me they were speaking another language! Carol couldn't wait to show Betty each particular animal, and, of course, my wife couldn't wait to get her hands on everything. She was petting wolves! . . . *Wolves!*" And I was! Carol was saying how wolves had always fascinated her, and I volunteered to send her a book on the subject, a volume I had just finished, *Arctic Wild* by Lois Crisler. (Carol has since founded the North American Wild Canid Society, devoted exclusively to the preservation and propagation of endangered wolves, and it thrills me when she says it was our conversation that day, plus the book I sent, that sowed the seed.)

Carol's response to our "thank you's," as Allen was finally dragging me away, was Carol at her best: She said, "What do people *do* who don't have a zoo?"

The whole zoo community has gone through a total metamorphosis since that summer of 1963. No longer is it a race between zoos to see which can exhibit the most extensive collection, with "one of everything" being the ultimate goal. It took a long while for zoo people to realize that that is a one-way street. It is no longer possible simply to turn around and replace animals from the wild population.

With shriveling habitats causing drastic reductions in the number of wild animals, and the endangered-species lists growing at such an alarming rate, it becomes increasingly imperative that zoos become producers, not consumers.

So it is, then, that the zoo community is playing an increasingly important role in trying to maintain some small hold on certain species before they slip away altogether. "Controlled captivity" seems to be the future for much of our wildlife; and there are those varieties today that exist *only* in zoos. The Père David's deer is a classic example. Had it not been for a captive herd maintained in China three hundred years ago, this lovely animal would have gone the way of the passenger pigeon . . . and so many others.

Today, bad zoos and so-called "roadside zoo" collections are being, albeit slowly, phased out. The major zoos of the world, rather than competing, are cooperating with each other in extensive breeding programs and animal management. This is not the two-by-two Noah's Ark approach, but a concerted effort to build up viable family groups of animals, through breeding loan programs and trade-offs from zoo to zoo. This makes sense from an animal-perpetuation standpoint, and gives the zoo visitor a more representational exhibit. No longer are zoos strictly in the business of public entertainment. . . . They have a job to do.

The major zoos today are also specializing more and more, emphasizing their strengths, rather than trying to be all things to all people. Each zoo has its own personality. Here are some of my favorites, and my reasons why:

At our National Zoo in Washington, D.C., Dr. Theodore Reed has his ongoing soap opera with the two giant pandas, a gift from the Republic of China. Pandas are notoriously hard to mate, and the course of true love has not run smoothly for Hsing Hsing and Ling Ling. It could be that after seven years of trying, patience will finally pay off—with a little artificial insemination help from their friends. By the time this book hits the stands, we'll know whether or not America is going to have its first native-born panda.

In Cincinnati, Ed Maruska has made his dream into a reality by creating the wonderful and unique World of Insects. Housed in a building of its own, the exhibit is like a fantasy world. There are jewel-box displays of exotic, dragonlike creatures which seem to belong on some other planet but were actually taken from a Cincinnati backyard. After seeing the exhibits in the World of Insects, my attitude and interest in them has altered completely; perhaps not quite to the point of a human/insect bond . . . but I have come a long way from George in his web over my front door.

Cincinnati has also had great success in breeding lowland gorillas. That is good news for all zoos around the world. The gorilla in the wild is seriously endangered, and even in captivity, his hold on the future is tenuous.

It was at the Columbus Zoo in Ohio in 1957 that the very first baby gorilla ever born in captivity was delivered, assisted by Dr. Warren Thomas, now director of the Los Angeles Zoo. Captive-born animals often do not reproduce, so it is wonderful news that the first baby's *granddaughter* is a healthy specimen. She is only *half* third generation, but certainly a step in the right direction. (I had the privilege of holding her when she was a tiny baby.)

Chicago's Lincoln Park Zoo, under the leadership of Dr. Les Fisher, has also had a fine gorilla-breeding program for several years. Dr. Fisher is heading up a symposium, funded by a grant from the Morris Animal Foundation, on "Breeding of the Great Apes in Captivity." The subject has such a high priority that the meetings will attract prime zoo people from around the world. The problem to be seriously addressed is *third* generation reproduction and beyond.

It was at Lincoln Park a few years ago that the first successful cornea transplant was performed on a Bengal tiger, with both veterinary and medical doctors officiating. This "meeting of the minds" is occurring more and more, with the realization that each has something to learn from, and contribute to, the other.

The Arizona Sonora Desert Museum near Tucson celebrates the animals indigenous to the area . . . the great Southwest on down into Mexico and Central America. "Visitors who come from out of town," says the local curator, "often know more about African animals, but they've

never seen any of the local fauna." Many times, zoos re-
frain from naming their animals for fear of overhumanizing
them, but sometimes the keepers can't resist. It was here in
Tucson that I saw "Gregory Peccary" and "Olivia de
Havalina" (a small wild pig of the area. . . . *No* aspersions
implied), and "Dolores del Burro." ("Ferret Fawcett" I
met at the Detroit Zoo.)

The San Diego Zoo is now working very closely with
the condor program of the Los Angeles Zoo in a desperate
last-ditch effort to save the giant California condor from
extinction. These magnificent birds have not changed since
prehistoric times, except, alas, in numbers. Ten years ago,
there were forty-eight birds in the wild . . . at last count the
number had dwindled to twenty.

About thirty miles north of the San Diego Zoo is its
Wild Animal Park. Here, in the relatively recent nonzoo
tradition, the animals roam free while the visitors ride in a
silent monorail train around the periphery of the park.
They get an overview of hundreds of acres of open country,
where the deer and the antelope play . . . with white rhi-
noceros and giraffe.

Another evidence of the changing face of the modern
zoo is the proliferation of drive-through animal parks
throughout the country. Their popularity attests further to
the public's interest in the wild ones.

Petting zoos exist in many animal parks. This is generally an area fenced off by itself, filled with pygmy goats,
sheep, llamas, and various and sundry other animals willing
to hold still for an army of little people bent on tactile contact. Some zoos even go so far as to post signs: NO ADULTS
ALLOWED UNLESS ACCOMPANIED BY A CHILD. These
areas should be monitored carefully, if inconspicuously, to
protect all concerned, whether they have two legs or four,

just as it is mandatory to let the animals take a break in a getaway place where they can't be followed.

There's an increasing tendency to use farm animals for these petting situations. Children, particularly those from large, metropolitan areas, are thrilled at getting close to animals they have previously seen only in picture books. In Central Park Zoo, New York, one of the exhibits is *bos bovis*—the domestic cow.

Through the years, I've had the pleasure of watching our Los Angeles Zoo grow into one of the world's finest. Don't take my word for it . . . come see us. And when you visit our beautiful new Koala House, stop to rest a moment in the Allen Ludden Plaza, made possible through gifts from his friends.

Los Angeles and San Diego are the only two zoos in the world where koalas can be seen outside of their native Australia. Our six were a bicentennial gift to Los Angeles from Australia, and we were ecstatic when three promptly had babies.

It is some indication of the human/animal bond that while koalas can be found only in Australia and California, and the giant panda is probably the rarest of animals . . . children around the world recognize both instantly and take them, literally, to their hearts.

Children and zoos, of course, are inseparable—but not simply for entertainment purposes. Another prime purpose by which a zoo justifies its existence is education. Classes arrive every morning on field trips and leave with enough material for school projects to carry them through the whole term.

The human-for-animal fascination, certainly one facet of "the bond" extends even to those whose physical or mental disabilities would seem to preclude it.

At LA Zoo there is an Exceptional Children's Program that is itself exceptional. In talking with Rosemary Deasy, who is deeply involved with this program—called Sharing the Zoo—I was struck by the similarity of her conversation to those we heard when sponsors of the therapeutic-horseback riding programs were speaking of the exceptional children. The words were almost identical, describing the joy of working with these people: "They are such *loving* people . . . they want to hug and kiss."

Rarely are there behavior problems encountered with these young people. They have worked for points to earn the privilege of coming to the zoo, so they are happy to be there. Teachers and aides and parents accompany them, so the zoo docent can concentrate on instruction. The name of the game here is patience . . . and the positive approach. It is "Pet the bird gently," *not* "We don't do that!"

There is a summer program designed to maintain mental stimulation for handicapped children who can't go to camp and don't have school to keep them alert. Sally Bower explained that "one docent is assigned four children, and as the same team works together all summer, they become a very personal unit." Because some of the students are deaf, *everyone* is taught to sign. For the blind, kits are prepared, including wool, washed and unwashed to show the difference in texture, a snake's shed skin, to show the feeling, and then of course, there is tactile contact with the live animals.

When the Exceptional Children's Program was instituted, it was assumed it would be just that—for children. However, in the past few years, the project has grown to include adults, some blind, some deaf, some deaf/blind—primarily senior citizens.

Deaf/blind groups, say the docents, are an exhilarating experience for all concerned, usually conducted by those docents who are trained in sign language, assisted by those who perhaps are not. Since the deaf/blind depend on touch to communicate, the docents are instructed to help guide a hand to pat the animals, and to squeeze a hand or an arm in response to a comment, since a smile will go unseen.

With the deaf/blind, the tour is one on one, with a docent for each individual. Carrots are distributed to the visitors to feed the elephant as they experience this huge animal. Rosemary Deasy said the questions are always "How big?" She repeated a conversation that she said was typical:

"How big? This big?"

"Bigger."

"*This* big?"

"Bigger."

"THIS big?"

"If you stretched up your hand as high as you could, you couldn't reach his eye!"

"Oh, dear, you won't let go of my hand, will you?"

Similar amazing interaction takes place when these people come to "see" our gigantic Clydesdale horse, Clancy, standing next to our tiny miniature horse, Princess. Clancy seems to feel their innocence and lets them feel him all over . . . even to the extent of putting their hands in his mouth. Clancy wouldn't dream of letting any "normal" person take such liberties.

When signing to deaf/blind, the docents do finger-signing . . . spelling out letters on the visitor's hand. These people read so fast that as part of a word is signed, they will keep pushing on in their eagerness to "hear" more.

The key to taking these exceptional visitors through the zoo is *simplicity*. The docents are told to talk with gestures and facial expressions when they do speak, but that it is not necessary to *talk all the time*. Give the visitors a chance to just look . . . or experience. . . . Excellent advice, applicable to those without disabilities as well.

Going through a zoo can be a most rewarding experience for everyone if, of course, (a) it's a good zoo, and (b) one approaches it with an open mind. For me, the best way to enjoy a zoo is to wander through alone, with no set compulsion to "see everything." Spending an hour in front of one exhibit when the animals are active can be fascinating and instructive. You not only learn a lot about the animals, but can get a good idea about the *people* watching the animals.

What constitutes a person's rapport with animals? Is it lack of fear . . . great respect . . . genuine affection . . . or a combination of all three? Or is it simply another manifestation of the human/animal bond at work?

I mentioned earlier my dream of being a keeper at a zoo. I wasn't kidding . . . it was neck-and-neck between that and forest ranger. In those days, my gender pretty well precluded both.

Now, of course, there are scores of women keepers around the country, and Ed Alonso, chief keeper at the LA Zoo, cannot speak highly enough of those on his staff. Dr. Warren Thomas told me once that in some cases, a woman's instinctive reaction—to hold an animal close . . . heartbeat to heartbeat—can be of the greatest help, especially with an ill or frightened or very young animal.

I asked Ed Alonso what he really looks for in a good keeper, once all the initial requirements are satisfactory on an application. His answer: "Generally, anybody can do the basic work, hauling hay, and cleaning out corrals and hosing down enclosures. But what we really look for is someone who understands animals, who can *read* a group of animals. And this is something hard to evaluate from a resumé or a brief interview. That's why we have a six-month probation period . . . by then we know how they are around the animals."

He also made the point that this was really not something that could be taught—either it's there or it isn't. Having this quality, however, can allow a keeper to sense, or "read," if an animal is under the weather long before any tangible symptoms appear. It also comes in very handy when dealing with volatile wild animals . . . in close quarters . . . on a daily basis.

There is one man I know who possesses this quality to a marked degree. His name is Bob Wolf, and for many years his particular charges have been the gorillas at our zoo. His awe of, and his love and respect for, these magnificent creatures are something to behold. I have seen him approach a mother gorilla whose newborn was jealously cuddled in her arms. Quietly, he congratulated her, and she relaxed visibly . . . to the point where her arms opened just enough for the baby to be seen. Bob's voice is low and soft, and he speaks reassuringly to the gorillas when he is introducing them to anyone . . . and that is just what he does . . . *introduces* them quietly to strangers.

I have often thought, watching Bob, that whether or not they understood the actual words, the gorillas must respond to being treated with such deep respect. They must also profoundly appreciate anyone who understands the value of a quiet approach. Their natural world is not a noisy one.

It is not unusual for great friendships to exist between keeper and charge, particularly when dealing with any of the great apes, and as a result, the most dangerous moment around a gorilla may not be when entering the enclosure, but when it is time to leave. Not aggression, but affection, many times, can spell trouble. A gorilla who has tolerated having a man in his compound cleaning and distributing food, breaking the monotony of his day, may, without realizing his own strength, try to keep his friend from leaving. Maintaining a critical distance is a good rule for any keeper in this situation, but it's difficult to keep a friend at arm's length when his arms are longer than yours!

Everyone with common sense and a basic instinct for self-preservation should have a healthy respect for animals, when it comes to approaching them . . . and let the animal set the tone. Reaching out rashly, whether to a chihuahua or to a lioness, can be asking for trouble. Some people are too smart to try it in the first place, while others are too dumb not to want to show off.

Somewhere between those two extremes are people who have such an affinity with animals that the animal senses it immediately and responds in kind. My friend Gene Wood (the voice you hear saying, "It's time for the Family Feeyewd!") has a daughter, Mia, so tuned in to horses that she can approach the spookiest of them with complete confidence. I have seen others who possess this mysterious brand of magic . . . to the degree that a dog, for example, who is usually stiff with strangers, will suddenly go boneless and adoring for no apparent reason when "that certain person" comes along. Even wild animals seem to sense this quality. They can also tell when it isn't there. . . .

Allen might not forgive me for telling this story, but I do so only to make a point.

We have all heard of psychosomatic pain, and doctors confirm that it can hurt just as much as pain from an injury or illness. One would expect to encounter this pain in any one of the institutions described in our earlier chapters. But hardly at the Catskill Game Farm!

The farm is a wild-animal facility situated in a lovely stretch of countryside north of New York City. Driving upstate, Allen, the three kids, and I stopped one afternoon to walk through the exhibits. They have varieties of hoofed stock, an assortment of birds, camels, llamas, ostriches . . .

We were in no hurry, and as we wandered through, each at his own pace, we became scattered. Suddenly Sarah came running back to say that Allen had been bitten by an ostrich. He was in great pain. I dashed up to see Allen, flanked by David and Martha, holding his hand and grimacing. Pacing back and forth at the wide-mesh fence was a huge male ostrich, obviously begging for a handout.

After looking at Allen's hand to make sure it was OK, I put my hand up to the fence, and the ostrich snapped at my fingers—once, then again. Once he had satisfied himself that I had no goodies to hand out, he stalked away in disgust.

Please believe that I wasn't being a smart aleck. It was just that I happened to know that an ostrich doesn't hurt you with his beak; his bite constitutes nothing more than a mild pinch. (It's those raking *feet* that have to be watched!) Allen didn't know that, so when the bird nipped his fingers, Allen's mind told him it must hurt . . . so it did! We all laughed, finally including Allen, and "ostrich" became an inside family joke forever.

Rapport with animals is really a matter of attitude. J. Allen Boone said it so eloquently in his *Kinship with All Life*. He tells of trying to trace down the folklore belief that rattlesnakes will strike at a white man but rarely at an American Indian. It is Boone's contention that the white man's ingrained attitude of fear and hatred toward the snake precedes him in any encounter; whereas the Indian can pass by the snake and each go on his way without hostility . . . simply respecting each other's place in the scheme of things.

Another example of mental attitude: One week we had Jim Nabors on *The Pet Set.* Since Jim was partial to white dogs, we did everything to please him . . . we had a flurry of white Samoyeds of all ages, along with a full sled team of Siberian huskies, and we dressed the set all in snow and pine trees . . . Jim loved it.

Each week, our friend Ralph Helfer from The Gentle Jungle Animal Compound would bring one or more of his movie animals into the studio for a short segment on the show. We had asked Jim ahead of time if there was any particular animal he would prefer seeing up close. "Heck no," said Gomer Pyle, "I love 'em all . . . 'ceptin' maybe snakes." The "'ceptin'" was an open invitation to Ralph Helfer, an avid herpetologist, who hoped to gain a convert. He brought in several different snakes, all carefully caged, and as he led Jim from cage to cage, Ralph described how really delicate and fascinating snakes are. Jim wasn't buying it.

Finally, as he was saying good-bye at the end of the interview, Ralph unbuttoned his shirt and kept unwinding a six-foot boa constrictor that had been quietly coiled around his body the whole time he had been talking to Jim. Jim turned white and backed out of the set and almost out of the studio—and even show business! We didn't change his attitude toward snakes one iota.

Ralph and I have been friends for over thirty years, going back to when he would bring beautiful macaws, which he raised in his backyard, to the first regular program I ever did, *Hollywood on Television,* which grew from *The Al Jarvis Show.* Through the years Ralph has become a highly successful trainer of animals for motion pictures and television.

It was Ralph, along with his beautiful wife, Tony, who probably first made me aware that the human/animal bond extended to wild animals, when he described his "affection training" program for performing animals. The accepted training method when Ralph was starting out was to make an animal perform through fear. Ralph said he got tired of being sent to the hospital by one rebellious animal or another, who was "just waiting for you to make one mistake." When Ralph acquired animals of his own to train, he opted for the reward system, and lots of hands-on affection. The animals responded in kind, and not only can Ralph now handle his animals but they are dependable with other people as well.

Performing animals have staked a large claim on the human/animal bond by helping raise the animal consciousness of young and old for generations.

Even many zoos today, whose policies have been adamantly against "animal shows," are changing their thinking. They are realizing that it is imperative to reach out and attract new visitors—once inside to see the show, these people will be exposed to all the rest of the good things a zoo has to offer.

The major consideration concerning performing animals is how they are trained, treated, and maintained. Today it is possible to receive a college degree in Animal Behavior and Operant Conditioning at Moorpark College in Ventura County, California, where an in-depth course is offered in Exotic Animal Training and Management. Under the direction of program director William Brisby and his wife, Diane, EATM (!), as it is known to participants, has placed graduates in animal-related jobs all over the country. Out of three hundred applicants, only sixty are accepted each year, most of whom are women who come from all over the United States.

The course lasts two and a half years, and during the first year the students only observe, feed, and clean the animals. By the second year, they are into a hands-on training program, and they are also supervising freshmen.

The 300 animals in the compound represent 143 species and come from a variety of sources. Some are on loan from the Los Angeles Zoo. There are also guest lecturers from various fields sharing their experiences as professional animal trainers, zoo directors, etc.

This school is indeed one of a kind. Today veterinary schools are also offering courses in wild-animal medicine for tomorrow's zoo vets.

With all these recent developments in the care and management of exotic animals, it would appear we have latched onto something new. Far from it. . . . Man's fascination with exotic animals goes back to the dawn of history, and he has long been an avid collector, exhibitor, and exploiter.

Still, compelling as they are, wild animals must never be confused with household pets. The aching desire to have one of these beautiful creatures for one's very own must be doused with the cold water of logic. Those who insist on taking nature into their own hands by adopting exotic pets are buying horrendous problems for themselves, and ultimate tragedy for the animals involved.

There is a newspaper clipping in my file—one of many similar—that includes a photo of a beautiful lion cub that had been adopted by a family of humans. The gist of the article is that the family had come to consider the cub to be a dear friend and pet—until one day when Mama Human came by his enclosure and he bit off her finger. End of friendship. The people just didn't realize that the cub was completely out of his proper environment. Who is to say what set him off? That was absolutely the wrong place for him.

People with monkeys encounter similar problems. Monkeys seem to fall on a borderline; nobody thinks of them as wild animals. They are considered pets. But anybody who buys a monkey is taking on more of a responsibility than one who adopts a child. They have all the neuroses that people do, plus a passionate need for *constant* companionship—and a boy monkey is better than a wrecking crew any day. It takes a certain kind of personality and a total commitment to maintain these adorable characters. Unfortunately, not many people can fulfill these requirements, and there are now several organizations devoted solely to caring for monkeys whose owners found they just couldn't cope.

There have been some attempts to train monkeys, capuchins in particular, to act as an extra pair of hands for paraplegics. The monkeys can be trained for the short term, but their personalities are not conducive to maintaining the assistance without constant reinforcement; this makes them impractical for such a program, and apt to bring more chaos than consolation.

Occasionally, I'll receive a letter that runs something like this: "I have a cougar and my landlord doesn't want me to keep him anymore. I'm in an apartment, you see. I know I shouldn't have taken him; guess I got a little tight that night." Unfortunately, it is only the cougar in this situation who winds up behind bars.

Sometimes, of course, people adopt wild animals almost by accident. A woman wrote to me once about Slugger, a young raccoon she had rescued. For two years he had been part of the family, having the run of the garage at night and even access to the rest of the house during the day. Slugger, unfortunately, grew up and didn't want that sort of life anymore. He bit members of the family, but the woman didn't want to take him to the local zoo because she thought the cages there would be too confining. She didn't want to turn him loose, because she lived in an area where raccoon hunting was a big sport. Poor Slugger! Ultimately, we were able to find a new home for him at a zoo—but that was just luck. Most zoos are inundated with such requests, and the standard answer is necessarily no.

The term "critical distance" means the point at which, when approached, an animal must make the choice between flight and aggression. All animals come equipped with this flashpoint to some degree. If the human/animal bond is strong within us, we will be willing to forgo trying to own one of these beautiful wild creatures, and we'll leave them in the care of professionals . . . so that we can continue to enjoy them at that "critical distance."

As Loretta Swit would say, this is the way to wear leopard.

No jokes, one of my great and dear friends, Major.

I won't neck with just anyone!

Jimmy and Gloria Stewart
visited *The Pet Set* with
their golden retrievers,
Simba and Bo . . .

. . . and Mary Tyler
Moore brought her
poodles, Maude and
DisWilliam.

There's a lot of love going on here . . . as Doris visits *The Pet Set*. (PHOTOGRAPH BY ROY CUMMINGS)

Whatever the future holds for me, animals (like Vin Melca's Before Dawn, a Norwegian elk hound) will be part of it. . . .

10.

Among Friends

In ancient Rome, when Androcles pulled the thorn from the lion's paw, he set up a chain reaction that ultimately saved his life. That was not his initial motivation, however . . . he was merely trying to ease the pain of a fellow creature.

This same compassion on the part of certain individual human beings has existed throughout history. How many people there are who are willing to extend themselves on behalf of species other than their own depends largely on what the current attitude-of-the-day toward animals happens to be. Sometimes it goes beyond the individual.

Old custom in rural areas of certain European countries provided that on Christmas Eve, no one ate until the animals were specially fed . . . a gesture of gratitude for their help throughout the year. These, of course, were working animals.

In India, some cattle are considered sacred, and roam at will, unmolested. Ancient China and Tibet cherished their small "lion dogs" and guarded them jealously from the outside world. Once upon a time, only royalty could bestow them as gifts to royalty.

At our present point in time, awareness of animals is on the rise. We worry about vanishing species in the wild,

218

and our pets have become a significant influence in our society for both owner and nonowner alike.

Working in television is not unlike living in a small town; when I mention one friend or another, it is often someone we all know. It will come as no surprise that of my personal friends in show business, a great many are devoted and active supporters of animal causes. They are never too busy to give of their time, their finances, and their energies to help wherever they can.

It is interesting to notice by what completely different routes we each approach the same goal, but no matter which way we choose to take, we all share one common "bond"—a deep and abiding concern for animals.

Many times, as you will see, the characters portrayed by these people on the screen are a far cry from their private-life enthusiasms. . . .

Doris Day. Mention animal enthusiast and Doris's name will come up in the same paragraph. She now lives in Carmel, California, with her troupe of dogs and cats. If you wish to get an accurate account of *just* how many she has in residence, Doris changes the subject. Moving through her beautiful home, I was happily surrounded by Biggest, and Autumn (sometimes called Autie Murphy for short), Bubbles (aka Varmint), Chipper (who also answers to C-h-h-o-p-p-p-e-e-Day), Schatzi, Heineken, Barney Miller, Trixie, Honey, Snowy (who cries and is afraid of the dark), and Bucky. These are a few of the dogs. Then, of course, there are the cats . . . Mr. Lucky, Miss Lucy, and Sneakers, a few others who preferred not to be introduced, plus Joey, a bird she is carefully nursing back to health. With each pet having a name and a nickname, it was a little tricky to keep count, but I came up with a ballpark figure of dogs, sixteen; cats, five; and bird, one.

Doris pours a lot of heart and money into her nonprofit Doris Day Pet Foundation, boarding out the animals that she finally *can't* handle at home. Lack of funds limits the number of animals that the foundation can take in, but the lucky ones get a truly new lease on life. So rescue and placement is the route Doris takes in animal support.

When I asked her the obvious question, "Have you always been hung up on animals?," Doris's answer surprised me. She said she had always loved them, but that her earlier days on the road as a band singer had made pet ownership a problem. It was not until she read J. Allen Boone's *Kinship with All Life* that she became so deeply committed. I have heard those words so many times from such different people; that is a very powerful book.

Doris uses her celebrity to help the animals she loves whenever she can. She has made records, the proceeds of which go into the foundation, and has spread the word in countless interviews. Nothing makes her angrier, after agreeing to an interview to further the animal cause, to have the interviewer go straight for "What is Rock Hudson really like?"

Doris is very eloquent when she describes what her animal family means to her: "[It] has been a source of joy and strength to me. I have found that when you are deeply troubled there are things you get from the silent devoted companionship of your pets that you can get from no other source.

"I believe they are here on earth to teach us. They have taught me to be patient, and they have taught me about love . . . fundamental love, such as Jesus taught.

"And loyalty. I have never found in a human being loyalty compared to that of any pet."

Loretta Swit. The lady herself bears small resemblance to Hot Lips Hoolihan, with whom we laughed and cried for twelve years of TV's *M*A*S*H*. Loretta is deeply serious in her fight for environmental concerns, working against whaling, seal slaughter, leg-hold traps, etc. She is especially vocal about the wearing of real fur, and practices what she preaches by looking smashing in the imitation variety. Loretta makes the point that no one appreciates the look, and above all, the *feel* of fur more than an animal lover (aside from the status connotation); however, there are too many available alternatives to justify the pain and loss of life involved. Loretta shares her home with five tiny, adorable dogs, most of them Pekingese. There is also a peke-a-poo or two, but I'm not one to gossip. . . .

Jimmy and Gloria Stewart. Gloria is a fellow trustee at the Los Angeles Zoo and enlists Jimmy's services at every opportunity. Both Jimmy and Gloria are deeply interested in all animals, wildlife in particular. Their daughter, Kathy, is following the same interests, and then some. Kathy works in the field in Africa with Dian Fossey, one of the world's leading authorities on gorillas in the wild. Gloria and Jimmy are justly proud of their daughter. Even in the midst of harrowing political unrest, the gorilla studies continue, in an effort to learn more about this wonderful creature that is in such jeopardy. So the Stewarts have found still another road to take in the interest of animals.

Earl Holliman. Actor, theater owner, businessman, president (of Actors and Others for Animals), Earl wears a lot of hats well, without short-changing any. Rugged personality though he portrays on the screen, Earl is a real soft touch where animals are concerned, and manages to devote almost as much time to them as he does to his career. Actors and Others has several strong suits—animal rescue and placement, pet population control—and it was very active in California in the fight to replace the old decompression method with euthanasia by injection. A strict vegetarian, Earl has a tremendous respect for life in any form. Or, I should say, forms. . . . He lives with wall-to-wall dogs and cats.

Gretchen Wyler. A Broadway dancer and television actress, Gretchen spends most of her energies working on behalf of the Fund for Animals. When she left New York, where she had worked so hard for the SPCA, and moved to California, she immediately involved herself in several statewide issues, which she fought for at the political level in Sacramento. She, along with Senator David Roberti, pushed through the Animal Bill of Rights, and, at this writing, they are very close to getting a law passed against pet-pound seizure for laboratory research. So the way that Gretchen has chosen to follow in our mutual interest is through political action.

Bob Barker. In explaining his feelings for animals, Bob says, "It's a case of puppy love that got out of hand." Although he has been partial to bassets, Bob and his late wife, Dorothy Jo, were both good friends of all animals for years, and always had a houseful of "just one mores." Bob lost Dorothy Jo not long ago, and she is missed by all of us. Bob works especially hard for the Los Angeles SPCA and often spreads the good word for animal welfare on *The Price Is Right* . . . and anywhere else the opportunity presents itself. The pets that he has rescued and brought such comfort to now have a chance to return the favor.

Edith Head. Cats could have had no better friend than designer Edith Head. Winner of a record eight Academy Awards for costume design in motion pictures, Edith gave wherever she could on the behalf of animals. Her interest was primarily cats, but not exclusively. At the time of her death in 1981, she and I were putting together a fashion/ animal show in Hawaii for the benefit of the Morris Animal Foundation. We went ahead with the show and dedicated it to Edith, and in her honor the turnout was even better than expected.

The light of her life was Gainsborough (lovingly known as Mr. Blue), a Russian Blue cat. At the time of her death, Mr. Blue was taken by Edith's great friend Roddy MacDowall.

Roddy MacDowall. When we speak of Lassie we must remember the movie that started it all, starring Roddy. I asked him about his working with this "dream dog," and he said, "Even with all the animals I've dearly loved since, I have never encountered quite the feeling I had for Lassie. He (yes, *he*) was so incredibly intelligent, and he had such *awesome* powers of concentration. And then he was so lovable and affectionate."

When the picture was finished, Roddy didn't want to part with his beautiful new friend and was furious that he couldn't keep the dog and live happily ever after.

Jock and Betty Leslie-Melville. Jock is British, Betty is American, and together they have lived in Africa most of their married lives. Also together, they founded the African Fund for Endangered Wildlife (AFEW).

Although proclaiming not to have been lifelong animal lovers (animal-*likers,* yes, but more interested in the political machinations in Africa), they became concerned about the dwindling herd of rare Rothchild's giraffe that were being crowded off the planet. They decided to do something about it. They generated a massive relocation effort, whereby a number of these animals were moved and set up in small nucleus herds elsewhere. In the course of this operation, Jock and Betty found themselves surrogate parents to first one baby giraffe, Daisy, and later a second, Marlon. These would-be non-animal-lovers went through horrendous growing pains until both babies reached maturity. Daisy and Marlon have both been full grown for some time now, and free to go off into the world. Instead, they remain in the vicinity and bring their wild friends home to meet the family. There are now *seven wild giraffe* that Jock and Betty can approach and touch.

There is also Walter, the wild warthog they found caught in a snare. Short-tempered by nature, Walter was in no mood to make friends, but by the end of six months of recuperation, when he was released, he kept coming "home" on occasion to be hand-fed. Jock and Betty may not have started out to be animal lovers, but when they converted, they went whole hog. . . . Quite literally.

Mary Tyler Moore. Mary is honorary chairman of the Morris Animal Foundation, for which all of us associated with Morris are extremely grateful. Her support of animal causes has been no secret through the years. On one occasion, Mary went to Washington to testify at a congressional hearing against steel leg-hold traps. She told me later that any stage fright she had ever experienced was nothing compared to what she felt that morning. However, her conviction was stronger than her panic, and appear she did. *Caring,* I think, is the secret word here.

For all the show people mentioned here, there are many more working just as hard on behalf of animals. I have only mentioned those in my personal acquaintance.

While I don't know Stefanie Powers, her dedication to establishing a foundation for animals in Africa, to carry on the work of William Holden in that area, is well known. Watching her on television, her hands, gentle and strong, on any animal she comes in contact with, tells the whole story of her feeling for them.

Barbara Bel Geddes is another woman I admire for her genuine appreciation of animals. Barbara's father, she has said, was influential in that department. "He was a man who loved animals and who should have been a naturalist."

She, in turn, has passed this concern down to her own daughter, Betsy Lewis. Four years ago, Betsy founded a nonprofit organization called Lifeline for Wildlife, Inc., in New York State. Lifeline was formed to fill a need. There were no professional facilities that could rescue injured and orphaned animals, heal them, and then release them into the wild. Betsy believed it was a job that had to be done. She says, "We must not ignore the wild animals. I'll do anything I can to help. . . . I grew up in a very animal-oriented household. Mother's concern was very powerful and very consistent." Barbara is still helping by being honorary chairperson of Lifeline for Wildlife, and a major supporter. The result is that from a one-woman operation for years, Lifeline has grown into a service that handles up to three hundred animals at a time in two separate facilities. They have a well-equipped hospital, with incubators and surgical equipment, plus ten acres in Ellenville, New York, with outdoor animal compounds.

As for my own affiliation and involvements, you already know that the Los Angeles Zoo is a major interest, and I work with all of the aforementioned people and organizations whenever I can, on specific issues and activities. My main function, however, is as president of the Morris Animal Foundation (no connection with Morris the Cat). This is a national, nonprofit organization headquartered in Denver, Colorado, and devoted to improving the health of our companion animals, funding studies into specific diseases of dogs, cats, horses, and zoo-wildlife. For ten years I served as vice-president of the Canine Division, but perhaps because I kept nosing into all the other departments, they wound up making me president.

Morris Animal Foundation was founded in 1948 by a veterinarian, Dr. Mark L. Morris, Sr., who became concerned when he realized that there was no organization dedicated to the health problems of our companion animals. The first meeting of this embryo group took place among four people and one German shepherd—Dr. Morris, his wife, Louise, Dr. J. V. Lacroux, and Morris Frank with his guide dog, Buddy—the same Morris Frank we spoke of earlier as co-founder of The Seeing Eye, Inc. The organization was funded privately at first by Dr. Morris and originally called the Buddy Foundation. Today, it is a multimillion-dollar foundation, but while it accepts outside funds, it is still a family organization, with Dr. Mark Morris, Sr., now retired, being abetted by his son, Dr. Mark Morris, Jr., and his daughter, Mrs. Ruth Keesling. MAF's advisory board, board of directors, and officers all serve on a volunteer basis, and pay their own travel expenses.

I am proud to be associated with such a dedicated group of people. Much has been accomplished. Much has yet to be done.

There are undoubtedly many people and organizations I have neglected to mention. The world—and not just the show business world—is full of caring animal lovers. So may I say a heartfelt collective thank-you to all.

No matter which course we choose to travel in pursuing our animal interests, I'm sure the same reasoning motivates us all. If we are to reap all the pleasure and benefit that we get from our membership in the animal club, we must pay our dues.

Animals have a way of bringing out the best in us, which alone is worth the price of admission.

11.

Betty's Catchall

Every kitchen has one drawer that is a catchall; it holds all the things that you don't know what to do with, but that you don't want to discard either. I see no reason why a book cannot have a catchall chapter, particularly when we are studying as broad a subject as the human/animal bond.

This, then, is our catchall!

We keep mentioning that fish are a good choice as pets. "Pets" may not be the accurate word, as you wind up getting your hand wet. However, they are companion animals. Many times, fish are permitted where no other pets are allowed, and they still provide a contact with the natural world. And, as has been established, watching fish can be beneficial in lowering blood pressure and calming hypertension.

At the time I got hooked on fish (sorry!), I didn't know any of this. I became interested in tropical fish simply because they are so beautiful to look at. . . . They are also fascinating to watch. . . . They can also be addictive.

At one point in my life, I started with just one betta (Siamese fighting fish) in a one-gallon tank. He was so pretty I got another one, but since the males will fight to the death if they are in together, I had to get a second tank. *That* was so attractive that I became interested in a five-gallon community tank. Now the trick was finding which types of fish can live in harmony without devouring each other. I no sooner got this sorted out than I discovered my platys and swordtails were living in such harmony that they were having babies by the gross. The adult fish will eat the babies unless you separate them immediately, which, of course, meant more tanks. It got so bad that my dad would swear we had fish in anything that would hold water. Before he'd put cream in his coffee, he'd check to make sure there weren't baby fish in the pitcher. There came a time when I had to start phasing out the fish collection, but to this day, my eyes begin to glaze when I pass an aquarium store. It's hard to kick the habit entirely.

Allen was fond of saying he should have known what an animal nut he was marrying long before the fact. As he told it, we were taking a drive through the country one beautiful spring day on a little back country road. We hadn't known each other very long. We passed a brilliant green hillside studded with Black Angus cattle, and, jokingly, I said, "You never stop to let me pet the cows!" He took me at my word, put on the brakes, and backed up to where a beautiful Angus was grazing near a fence. By now it was a challenge, so, of course, I piled out and walked to the fence with outstretched hand. "She walks up to this one cow," Allen would say later, "and it comes over to be scratched! Well, from nowhere . . . from nowhere . . . these damn cows keep coming and pretty soon this woman is talking to eleven of them all lined up at the fence! I tell you, she's a little weird!"

It was a lovely moment, and it was fun to have him think I possessed some sort of mystique. The mundane fact of the matter—that he would never believe—is that the Angus were probably just curious.

There *is* an undeniable mystique that animals themselves seem to possess, an element that baffles animal lovers and scientists alike. One hears countless stories of dogs and cats, for instance, returning to their homes after incredible journeys over vast distances and great elapsed time. There is even a record of a two-year-old Brahman heifer making one of these journeys after she was sold by her owner to another cattle breeder thirty-five miles away. Finding herself penned in, she waited until after dark, jumped out of the pen, leaped over two four-foot barbed-wire fences, swam the Econlockhatchee River, forded several small creeks, and twenty hours later showed up at her old farm home. And she was carrying an unborn calf at the time. Unsurprisingly, after this, her original owner took her back and refunded the price of the sale.

The bond doesn't always manifest itself in such sensational ways. One incident in my personal acquaintance is another small example of that same quality. A good friend, Dona Singlehurst, who lives in Hawaii, is an avid animal lover and works very hard on their behalf. She had a dear otterhound, Waldo, who, in Hawaii's moderate climate, preferred to live outdoors. He was in the habit of accompanying his mistress on her customary morning horseback rides. One day, Dona was thrown from her horse and broke both of her feet. When she was carried home and put on the couch to wait for the doctor, Waldo nearly tore down the front door to get in and lie next to her on the couch. He remained her self-appointed guardian throughout her recuperation, and Dona tells of this big, shaggy dog lying so still beside her, with a kitten snuggled between his paws. When at long last his friend was up and around, Waldo could go back to being his old outdoor self.

That special insight that an animal has is also evident when he chooses one person above any other as his very own . . . many times with no connection as to who feeds him. I am convinced that there also exists an "animal/

companion human bond" . . . wherein their choices are as unfathomable to us as ours must be to them.

This often happens with a household pet, of course, but it can also occur under the strangest circumstances. One day I was filming a commercial on location in a lovely park on the outskirts of the city. It was for a bakery product, and to emphasize the freshness of the ingredients, they had me gathering newly laid eggs in the clear, sunny, early morning. To make the setting even more pastoral, a flock of white chickens was turned loose on the green lawn around me.

To put all these elements together took the better part of a day. When the chickens had first been released in the morning, of course, I was enchanted and talked to them immediately, but only casually, since I was busy with the job at hand. This was a flock of maybe twenty ordinary, untrained, garden-variety white Leghorn chickens, pecking at some scattered seed, strictly for atmosphere, while wranglers stood by on the sidelines shooing them back into camera range.

One chicken kept staying close to me, and as I moved, she would tag along. As the day wore on, it became obvious to everyone, and by the time we broke for lunch, she was sitting on my lap. The rest of the flock of "extras" wouldn't let me near them. By the end of the day I was vainly trying to figure a way to integrate this bird with the rest of my menagerie at home. As it was, we had to part, but I got the trainer's solemn vow that she would be kept as a pet, not put back with the others. Anyone who tries that hard to communicate must be appreciated.

Years later, when I was doing a guest shot on the television show *Fame,* the script girl, Sally Roddy, began telling me about her pet chicken. Madeleina, it seems, is another people-oriented bird. Sally found her one day, and when it became apparent that Madeleina had moved in to stay, Sally built her a house. Sally carries her around while watering the garden, the hen comes running when she

hears the shower, and she sits contentedly in the lap of
Sally's little girl. She also shares the birdseed put out with
all the other birds . . . except doves. She chases doves! As
a thank-you for all the tender loving care, Madeleina du-
tifully presents an egg a day.

Evidently, these poultry-person alliances aren't as unusual as I thought; both Sue Ane Langdon and Nanette
Fabray told me that they, too, have had chicken friends.

The name—human/companion animal bond—may be
of very recent vintage, but the bond itself has existed anon-
ymously throughout time. There is a wide variety of ways,
some better known than others, that animals have worked
together with humans, contributing certain physical qualities that man does not possess.

Dachshunds, for example, who were originally bred
long and low to be able to follow an animal in the field
down into its burrow, have found a new big-city job in Germany. They have been called upon to help string telephone
cable through narrow passages—just as ferrets have long
been used in England for pulling wire through conduits. In
the technologically sophisticated eighties, it was somewhat
surprising to learn that these little animals were actually
used in setting up the wiring for the worldwide coverage of
Prince Charles's wedding.

For a hundred years or more, people have been telling
stories of strange behavior on the part of their animals prior
to earthquakes. In Japan, the actions of goldfish have been
credited with actual earthquake predictions. China has been
doing some research in this connection, and for a time, so
were scientists in the United States. For about five years, we
had a federally funded program called Earthquake Watch in
operation. A network of about 1,500 people with dogs, cats,
horses, cows, birds, and fish was set up to report an unusual
behavior witnessed in their animals. The program was based
in California, since we are admittedly shakier than the rest

of the country, and while some relatively interesting results were tabulated, they were not conclusive enough to keep the program from running out of funds.

In Britain, a member of the British Parliament, Miss Janet Fookes, B.A., M.P., was enumerating all the ways that dogs work with and for their human companions. She concluded her list by saying, "And I think the most superb example of a dog trained for man and woman's need [is] what we call in Britain sniffer dogs, which are used either to sniff out drugs or to sniff out explosives. We have two delightful Labradors that go round the House of Commons half an hour before we sit every day, and I usually try to meet them. They go round to sniff out any sort of modern Guy Fawkes waiting to blow us up, and invaluable they are."

We are well aware of these stalwart sniffer dogs in this country, both as narcotics agents and valuable working members of any bomb squad. One variation I had not heard of before is the use of dogs as termite detectors. Trained beagles are reputed to be highly accurate, although not as cost-effective as traditional human inspectors. The dogs are able to identify only live colonies of termites and carpenter ants. They sniff along the baseboards, and when they find the culprits, they don't bark but scratch the baseboards and look at the trainer. It seems the dogs are able to smell certain "volatile materials" emitted by the termites, and to hear them chewing on wood. . . . With all this competition, no wonder bloodhounds look so worried!

No matter what kind of pets you may have, or how well you may think you know them, now and then they will do something utterly baffling. It may escape your notice once or twice, but if the aberration is consistent enough to catch your attention, they can have you talking to yourself.

My Timmy is four years old, and I am very high on his list of priorities. When he isn't actually at my heels, you can rest assured that he knows exactly where I am. I cast a very tiny, alert, black shadow. If we happen to be in different parts of the house or garden, I need only call his name once, and he checks in.

Get the picture?

Then explain this for me:

Every so often, the kitchen becomes a no-man's-land for Timmy. He will be bouncing at my heels until I reach the kitchen. I turn to look, and he is sitting in the dining-room doorway. No matter how I call, coax, or demand, he gets three sizes smaller, turns his head away, and won't even look at me. This is the same dog who came to get me a moment before and asked to be let out.

It is a complete stalemate until I pick him up and carry him to the other end of the kitchen, where he becomes bouncy, happy Timmy again, dancing out into the garden as if nothing had happened. I would think this was simply an attention-getting device (which are common, I'll admit), but he's never short of being held, and this only happens in the kitchen, and only sporadically.

Any ideas? There is a heat vent on the wall at floor level, but there is no heat on most of the year. We don't have air conditioning, so it isn't temperature-oriented, and it can happen any time of the day or night or season. Sooner is absolutely unaware of any of this and couldn't care less. Much of the time he is somewhere else in the house, so there is no subliminal dog language involved.

Now, none of this would be worth noticing if it occurred all the time. It would be easy to break the code. However, after a day or two at the most, it's back to business as usual, and the kitchen reverts to that place where dinner is prepared. It stays that way for two or three weeks, then, once again, suddenly it's the haunted house.

The only reason I am mentioning this is that I have read just enough about animal hallucinations to be fascinated. Also, when Tim is trying so hard to tell me something, I hate to be so *dense*.

While we are on the subject, I should tell you about Willie. When Allen and I were first married, we bought a 175-year-old farmhouse in Westchester County, New York, in the middle of an old apple orchard. The property had been carefully remodeled by the previous owners, with a real effort to retain as much of the old buildings as possible. They had moved the original little farmhouse back from the road, attached it to the old stone barn foundation, and built on from there. The walls were over a foot thick in some of the rooms, and sticking up into the attic over the third floor, intact, was the original farmhouse roof.

Well, we were enchanted, of course. Anyone would have been under the circumstances, let alone being madly in love, newly married, and incurably romantic by nature.

We moved into our dream house—the three children, David, Martha, and Sarah, plus the two chocolate poodles, Willie and Emma, and Allen and I. Not long after, we began to hear noises that couldn't be explained away by the growing pains of the old building. Again and again I would awaken to the sound of muffled laughter somewhere in the house. At first I thought it was the girls (David was away at school at Andover), but it continued to happen even when the girls went to summer camp. At first when I told Allen, he was ready to throw a net over me, but he finally heard it a few times himself. One night, I heard a woman's voice call out, "Jeb!?" (Jeb is not a name I'd be likely to make up).

We determined not to mention it to the housekeeper or the kids, in the event they might be uneasy. If they ever heard anything, they never told us.

The dogs were something else. Not so much Emma, but Willie, the boy poodle, was never one to keep a secret. Every once in a while, day or night, he would run for the foot of the front stairs, which had been part of the original farmhouse, and stand looking up, emitting a low growl. Nothing or no one could induce him up those stairs for the next hour or two; then everything would go back to normal

again for weeks on end. Willie *never* growled at any other
time in all the fifteen years of his life.

Healthy imaginations at work? No doubt. But now and
again I happen across something in my reading that makes
me wonder. What *was* Willie trying to tell us?

In Chapter Nine, we touched briefly on the subject of
performing animals—an umbrella term covering a wide variety of situations. There are those who have expressed
misgivings that any animal required to perform in any con-
text for purposes of entertainment is being exploited. In
response, I would like to zero in on the one small facet of
the subject with which I have had personal experience—
animal actors performing in motion pictures and television.

Before any other aspects are considered, of course,
Priority One must be how the animals are trained and
maintained during their "careers." The American Humane
Association has worked long and hard to establish humane
guidelines within which animal trainers must operate. AHA
headquarters are in Denver, but it maintains a busy Hollywood Office under the direction of Carmelita Pope, to
oversee all animal action in films and shows within their
jurisdiction.

Each year, AHA presents PATSY Awards (Performing Animals Top Star of the Year) for the best animal
performance achieved through training under approved humane standards. The Humane Society of the United States
is also active in maintaining these standards, as are all of
the top professional animal trainers in Hollywood.

Arguments against using animals as actors must be
weighed against the number of friends these performers have
made and continue to make for the animal kingdom. Strongheart, Rin Tin Tin, Trigger, Lassie, Rhubarb the cat, Ed the
talking horse, Benji, Boomer, Fred the cockatoo, even
grumpy old Morris . . . generations have grown up on them.

One school of thought is that they do not represent life

as it really is; ergo, it's wrong. If, indeed, dramatic license is taken, does it really do us all that harm? We *know* horses can't actually talk. We *know* Lassie can't solve every problem in the whole world, but there are people all over the globe who automatically smile at every collie they see, thanks to these programs. Is this fantasy world any more damaging than the epidemic of stark realism we have been going through of late? Are we honestly better off because those two mules in *Patton were* actually shot to death before our eyes? (Filmed overseas, *Patton* was out of American Humane Association jurisdiction.) Is it a must to kill sheep and chickens so they will bleed real blood? I think not. But to negate *all* performing animals is painting with too broad a brush.

It is just possible that the tremendous response to a little reptilian creature called E.T., whose problems were resolved with a happy ending, may be indicative that audiences are ready to be encouraged once again. Could it be that E.T.'s charm could have a remote relationship to the human/animal bond?

Before closing our "kitchen drawer," perhaps there is one loose end that should be tied up. Wherefrom T.K.?

For years I have been bemoaning the fact that much as I ached to have a cat in the family, Sooner had made it abundantly clear that he would not put up with it. But times have changed.

Ten months ago a beautiful black kitty staked out a claim at the back of my garden. Every day, for hours on end, he perched on a rock overlooking the ivy that grows down the hill, evidently a perfect vantage point for the professional hunter. To Sooner, the cat might as well have been invisible, which I couldn't blame completely on Soonie's advancing age, since he still chases squirrels with all his old passion.

At first, I was content to enjoy this visitor from a distance; but as time went by I couldn't resist trying to approach him. Fat and sleek and obviously belonging to someone in the neighborhood, he wanted no part of me. He would melt into thin air if I tried to get any closer than about ten feet . . . his "critical distance." However, if I stuck to my own business of picking flowers, he would behave as if I didn't exist. I tried picking closer and closer and kept my back to him, and as soon as I got to the ten-foot barrier, instead of disappearing, he would roll and talk and tease, always moving far enough away to keep that ten feet between us.

I cannot tell you what a complete fool I made of myself trying to back up imperceptibly to this animal who obviously couldn't care less. It became a matter of pride with me, and I wasn't going to give up on a challenge. Didn't this cat know that he was snubbing Miss Animal Lover, who, by reputation and word of mouth—hers—could eventually break down any animal's resistance? And this went on for almost three months.

Finally, out of utter frustration, I decided to play my trump card. Breaking a cardinal rule regarding feeding someone else's pet, I went back into the house and got a handful of dry cat food (left over from one of my unsuccessful attempts to integrate Sooner).

Armed with the goodies, I eased my way out to his domain, sat down on the grass at about the ten-foot line, and tossed a couple of pieces toward him. Well, he talked and he rolled, and went away, and came back a few times—he went through his whole number. Suddenly, as if a switch had been thrown, before my eyes this sultry Lorelei turned into a perfectly normal cat. He got up, walked unhurriedly to the two pieces of food, ate them, walked over to me and crouched over my open hand until he had leisurely eaten every bite. Then he jumped into my lap, and purring like an outboard motor, *demanded* to be loved.

When I finally pulled myself away, he followed me right up to the back door, ready to come in and take up residence. In this case, Sooner kept me honest, because while that well-fed kitty obviously belonged to someone, I would have been sorely tempted to "rescue" him.

After that, I could approach him at any time with no bribe involved, and it finally dawned on me that I had been had. That black devil had been putting me on, making me behave like an idiot, until he got me right where he wanted me. Pushy cat!

How I misread this lovely creature! It has been almost a year now since I first saw *her* in my garden. As I am scribbling this update, T.K. is sitting on my table, slapping at my pencil. By degrees, she has moved in and most of us have fallen completely in love. Sooner is still not thrilled, but he has learned to go to sleep with her in the room. My housekeeper, Betty Proctor, has also fallen under her spell. Betty will look into her eyes and say, "Well, T.K., I see the tide is still low!," explaining that her mother always told her that when the pupils of a cat's eyes were large and dark it meant the tide was running high.

When T.K. elected to take us on as a family, I took her for a checkup and discovered she is a spayed female, full-grown but kittenish enough to play a lot. She has evidently had dog friends, because she follows Timmy around like a groupie, even when he is tired of playing—hence the name, Timmy's Kitty. Her sweetness keeps increasing along with her confidence, and although she is still leery with strangers, I'm convinced she has known tender loving care. Did her family move away? Was she brought here and abandoned? Did she find her way back to an old stamping ground? I will never know. . . . I am just grateful that we found each other. The fact that she picked Hallowe'en to make her decision to move in seems a little much. Perhaps I should have called her Jeb!

12.

Wrapping Up . . . The Human/Animal Bond

There is supposedly an old rule in comedy: In building a funny situation, they say, "Tell 'em what you're going to do, do it, then tell 'em what you just did."

At the beginning of this book, I told you we were going to investigate the human/animal bond together. We did just that. And now, I, for one, would like to take a quick look at "what we just did." But believe me, this is no joke.

When I first started this project, I thought I knew a little about human/animal relationships, but I soon discovered my knowledge was at the kindergarten level. However, even the top authorities, who at this point know more about the human/animal bond than anyone, are, like Alice stepping through the looking glass, discovering a whole new landscape stretching out before them. And—one of the most exciting facets of this adventure—they are looking around to find other people from other related fields looking back at them.

In our research, we spoke to many people, heard and read diverse approaches to the subject of animals used in therapy. We have cited case after case from all over the world, and for every one we mentioned there were many more from which we had to choose. These case histories involved a variety of health problems, and certainly a wide assortment of animals. But what I found amazing was that no matter how divergent the individual situations—or how separated the geography—the results came out sounding as if they had been assessed by the same person. Even the language was almost identical. The response is undeniable.

At no time have pets been represented in these pages as the miracle cure-all that will take complete care of the ills of the world. What *is* being said here is that as an *adjunct*—as a contributing positive influence on our daily lives—animals have proven themselves invaluable to those of us inclined to be near them. Not only is their use in therapy for the disabled under close scrutiny, but their relationship to everyone in general is being examined . . . and taken very seriously.

The human/animal bond is something so tangible it can almost be held in the hand. It is a whole new source of energy. Like oil, it is a fossil fuel, in that both have been around since the dawn of history. Like water, the power of which can be harnessed to generate electricity, this bond we speak of, when properly channeled, can *also* be used to make things work.

Because we are all just on the threshold of examining this phenomenon, only now has the time finally arrived when all the divergent discoveries and opinions on the bond can be brought together for comparison and sifted down until some kind of pattern emerges.

In a recent dog-club publication, *Rhodesian Ridgeback,* I read something that suits this situation perfectly, although they were discussing a totally different subject. They said: "The first step is the sponge—the thirst for knowledge, the devouring of all written and spoken opinions without the wisdom of knowing what to reject."

One group, the Latham Foundation, has developed a computerized reference system to give researchers immediate access to the wide range of pertinent publications. This information source is invaluable, as it focuses on *all* aspects of the human/animal bond.

In 1979, the first meeting took place in which serious people sat down to talk about the various aspects of the human/animal bond. The meeting was held in Scotland and there were only a few people present . . . ten at the most.

The next meeting was held in London, with 300 in attendance. In October 1981, an International Conference on the Human/Companion Animal Bond was held at the University of Pennsylvania and attracted 450 people from many countries. Information was presented to health professionals, including physicians, veterinarians, nurses, social workers, and hospital and chronic-care-facility administrators. Also attending were animal-control officers, the humane community, animal trainers . . . *all* those in any line of animal-related endeavor.

A meeting held in Canada nine months later was followed by two more in the summer of 1983 in the United States, and yet another in Vienna in late autumn 1983 . . . each attracting more and more people and consequently receiving more varied input and generating far-reaching results.

Wherever all this is leading, it will be a fascinating progress to observe. It will also, of necessity, mellow some currently rigid attitudes in several schools of thought. Those working in humane-oriented activities, for example, have long been more or less on a collision course with the scientific community. Conversely, those of the veterinary-medical persuasion have looked askance at the "humaniacs" as being unrealistic and overemotional. By the very fact of meeting under one roof, being able to hear each other's problems and air their own, these people are finding—to their amazement—that many times they are interested in the same goals: the relationship of animals with people and the basic welfare of both.

Many times, as we have pointed out, a veterinarian is called upon to give advice to a pet owner that transcends his function as a vet. A delicate situation can and has developed on occasion, when a client brings in a pet, then opens up on problems of his own that he doesn't feel ready to discuss with his own doctor.

Dealing with human emotion and people's involvement with pets is, with increasing frequency, being built into the curricula of veterinary schools around the country. More emphasis is being placed on dealing with client grief at the loss of a pet, as well. What it amounts to is that veterinarians are finding that it's more difficult to deal with pets and owners as *separate* entities, and that it's more productive for all concerned not to try.

At the other end of the pendulum swing, those involved in humane work with animals are having to face some truths of their own as they continue to wage the battle with increasing numbers of unwanted pets. They are having to modify slightly some previous black-and-white opinions and accept some painful grays.

Heartbreaking as it is, the destruction of surplus healthy animals will continue until people finally get the message that *they* are the ones responsible. Even alternative methods of contraception, which will gradually become available, can be only as effective as those administering them allow them to be.

Identifying the human/animal bond expresses the fervent hope that more people will begin to realize the potential of how much animals can do for *us*, and will care for *them* accordingly.

It has always been my personal philosophy to *try* at

least to appreciate the moment in time in which I am standing. So often I hear people sigh, "I didn't realize how great that was at the time," or, "I can't wait till summer comes." For them, the *present* moment never seems to exist. Animals have no such sense of past or future. Perhaps it was the animals I love who have tried to teach me their wisdom . . . realize the now . . . for whatever it is.

Tom Watson caught my ear one time when he said, "Some people are 'hard of seeing!'" True. We are bombarded these days by such a constant barrage of negatives that we are beginning to tune them out. We can take just so many horror stories before we begin to build up emotional calluses for our own protection against the pain of others. We get so caught up insulating ourselves against the bad that the good stuff often slips by unnoticed, and, indeed, we do become "hard of seeing."

If and when that begins to happen, those of us with pets are fortunate to have our own in-house therapists. No special training equipment or degree is necessary for them to provide beneficial treatment . . . just regular short sessions of interaction, guaranteed to shake up one's sense of values.

We've spoken of the calming effect animals can provide to relieve hypertension. Let me tell you there's a lot of that going around when you're writing a book. Timmy and Sooner and T.K. sensed there was a job for them to do, and they stayed on duty throughout . . . always within reach. Many times, if I began to panic, they would distract me for a moment; then I would come back with a fresh outlook. Their names should really be on the cover. And now they will help me relax and unwind . . . an animal's work is never done!

The consensus among most sociologists today is that no human is self-sustaining or can live in isolation, but rather, we live in communities which include other species as well as our own. The involvement among these species is evident again and again in our case histories.

It would be impossible to choose, of all the stories we have heard, which is the most memorable. One, however, stays with me as a prime example of what the human/companion animal bond can mean throughout a long lifetime. When we were speaking about the Handi-Dogs Program, we mentioned one of the students, an eighty-eight-year-old woman who had trained her own two dogs, then returned to the program to work as a volunteer. Lillie Passano, who was ninety-six on May 1, 1983, says it better than anyone. She writes:

> I have often been asked the secret of my long, active life. My answer is: mental attitude and vitamins and minerals in late years, *and dogs always*.
>
> I lived through the Great Depression, during which my husband died tragically, a victim of it, in Phipps Psychiatric Clinic of Johns-Hopkins. That night a great psychiatrist, Thomas A. C. Rennie, said to me, "When you return to your job, some well-meaning person may advise you to change your way of living, involving disposing of your dogs . . . Don't do it!" The doctor said, "When you return from work to an empty house, those welcoming noses at the threshold of your door, waiting for your return, will mean a great deal to you." They did.

Lillie went on to say that one night before his initial heart attack, her husband was suicidally inclined and, leaving her with her dogs, went out of the house and into the cold and darkness. She recalls:

I was powerless, and feared the worst. This is what I did, with the aid of a dog: set out in the car, on a little-traveled back road, with a cocker spaniel beside me, till I saw, in the dim car lights, my husband leave the road. When I dared, I left the car in shrubbery and with the dog in my arms, lest crackle of undergrowth alert him that he was being followed, I approached the dreaded murky water, a deep drop from the surface.

Then I set the dog down very quietly with instruction, "Go find master."

Then, oh how welcome in the stillness, the word "Freckles." My husband evidently thought the dog had followed him from home. And his conversation with the dog was normal—totally unlike suicidal, discouraged pouring out of his own great depression. Soon, near ground level, where he had presumably sat down with the dog on a rock at the lake shore, the gleam of a lighted cigar. And I knew he was safe with the dog.

Dogs and what they can do have helped me greatly to "keep on going." . . .

Not long ago, Lillie suffered a paralyzing stroke when she was alone in her trailer home in Tucson. Her two little dogs, Yin and Yang, were the only witnesses. . . .

and by licking my face kept me conscious enough to alert phone operator from the dangling instrument. And those two small dogs—who had some Handi-Dog training, stood by, licking my face, till ambulance came.

This letter is part of what dogs have meant to me in 95 years.

That just about says it all.

I said it would take the space of this book to explain why I find it so difficult to separate people and animals completely in my mind. I also promised to be as objective as I could. Sorry . . . that is just not possible when the subject is love.

Appendices

APPENDIX A

The Latham Foundation

During the course of this book, we mention the Latham Foundation with some frequency, and we are deeply grateful for its assistance on this project.

Latham is not only in the vanguard of the human/animal bond (we've spoken of its setting up a central, computerized clearinghouse to amalgamate existing information), but was predicated on the bond. Edith Latham loved animals, cats particularly, one cat *most* particularly, and when she died, rather than do as many have done and will her fortune to that one cat (for all the interested parties to fight over), she chose to start a foundation to benefit all animals. For sixty-seven years now, the Latham Foundation has been working effectively in the field of humane education both here and abroad.

Latham may well be in the middle of its biggest effort to date in making people aware of human/animal bond research. Hugh Tebault, Latham's president, says, "In our opinion, failure to recognize, study, and employ the benefits of the human/companion animal bond as a highly significant, available, cost-effective resource, is to ignore a magnificent scientific breakthrough and to deny society a phenomenal new resource." Perhaps the good work it has accomplished so far can all be traced back to that one most particular cat . . . Edith Latham's friend, Pussywillow.

Directory

Following is a directory of many of the associations, schools, and institutions mentioned in this book, all of which are intimately involved with various aspects of the human/companion animal bond.

ASSOCIATIONS

American Animal Hospital Association
204 Lincolnway East
Mishawaka, Indiana 46544
(212) 256-0280

American Humane Association
9725 E. Hampden Avenue
Denver, Colorado 80231
(303) 695-0811

Canadian Council on Animal Care
151 Slater
Ottawa, Ontario K1P 5H3 Canada
(613) 238-4031

Center for the Interaction of Animals and Society
University of Pennsylvania
3800 Spruce Street
Philadelphia, Pennsylvania 19104
(215) 243-4695

Center to Study Human-Animal Relationships
    and Environments
University of Minnesota
1-117 Health Sciences Unit A
515 Delaware Street S.E.
Minneapolis, Minnesota 55455
(612) 373-8032

Doris Day Pet Foundation
Box 600
Beverly Hills, California 90213

The Delta Society
N.E. 1705 Upper Drive
Pullman, Washington 99163
(509) 335-9515

Humane Society of the Pikes Peak Region
P.O. Box 187
Colorado Springs, Colorado 80901
(303) 473-1741

Humane Society of the United States
2100 L Street N.W.
Washington, D.C. 20037
(202) 452-1100

Joint Advisory Committee on Pets in Society
117 Collins Street
Melbourne 3000, Australia

The Latham Foundation
Latham Plaza Building
Clement & Schiller
Alameda, California 94501
(415) 521-0920

Morris Animal Foundation
45 Inverness Drive East
Englewood, Colorado 80112
(303) 779-8867

Pets are Wonderful Council
500 N. Michigan Avenue, Suite 200
Chicago, Illinois 60611
(312) 836-7145

People-Pet Partnership Program
College of Veterinary Medicine
Washington State University
Pullman, Washington 99164
(509) 335-9515

Society for Companion Animal Studies
Animal Studies Center
Freeby Lane
Waltham-on-the-Wolds
Melton Mowbray
Leicestershire, LE14 4RT
United Kingdom
0664-64171

GUIDE-DOG SCHOOLS:

Guide Dogs for the Blind
350 Los Ranchitos Road
P.O. Box 1200
San Rafael, California 94902
(415) 479-4000

Guide Dog Foundation for the Blind, Inc.
109-19 72nd Avenue
Forest Hills, New York 11375
(212) 263-4885

International Guiding Eyes
13445 Glenoaks Boulevard
Sylmar, California 91342
(213) 362-5834

Leader Dogs for the Blind
1039 Rochester Road
Rochester, Michigan 48063
(313) 651-9011

Pilot Dogs, Inc.
625 W. Town Street
Columbus, Ohio 43215
(614) 221-6367

The Seeing Eye, Inc.
P.O. Box 375
Morristown, New Jersey 07960
(201) 539-4425

HEARING-DOG SCHOOL:

Hearing Dog Program
The San Francisco SPCA
2500 16th Street
San Francisco, California 94103
(415) 621-1700

ASSISTANCE-DOGS SCHOOLS:

Canine Companions for Independence
P.O. Box 446
Santa Rosa, California 95402
(707) 528-0830

Feeling Heart Foundation
RFD 2, Box 354
Cambridge, Maryland 21613
(301) 228-9407

Handi-Dogs, Inc.
P.O. Box 12563
Tucson, Arizona 85732
(602) 326-3412

Support Dogs for the Handicapped
5900 N. High Street
Worthington, Ohio 43085
(614) 436-5345

EQUESTRIAN THERAPY PROGRAMS:

Ahead With Horses, Inc.
9311 Del Arroyo Street
Sun Valley, California 91352
(213) 767-6373

Cheff Center
8479 N. 43rd Street
Augusta, Michigan 49012
(616) 731-4471

North American Riding for the Handicapped
 Association, Inc.
P.O. Box 100
R. 1, Box 218
Ashburn, Virginia 22011
(703) 471-1621

PRISON PROGRAMS:

Lima State Hospital for the Criminally Insane
Drawer Q
Lima, Ohio 45802
(419) 227-4631

Purdy Prison Partnership Program
Veterinary Science 110
Washington State University
Pullman, Washington 99164
(509) 335-9515

SCHOOLS/TRAINING TO WORK WITH WILD ANIMALS:

Exotic Animal Training and Management Program
Moorpark College
Moorpark, California 93021
(805) 529-2321

Read More About the Bond

Following is a list of books and publications, some of which served as source material for this book but all of which will provide interesting "further reading" for those so inclined. This is by no means meant to be an exhaustive list.

Beal, Louisa, and Linda Hines. *Annotated Bibliography of the People-Pet Partnership Resource Library*. Alameda, Calif: Latham Foundation.

Beck, Alan, and Aaron Katcher. *Between Pets and People*. New York: Putnam's, 1983.

Boone, J. Allen. *Kinship with All Life*. New York: Harper & Row, 1954.

Bustad, Leo K. *Animals, Aging and the Aged*. Minneapolis: University of Minnesota Press, 1980.

Caras, Roger. *A Celebration of Dogs*. New York: Times Books, 1982.

Corson, Samuel, and Elizabeth O'L. *Ethology and Non-Verbal Communication in Mental Health: An Interdisciplinary Biopsychosocial Exploration.* Elmsford, N.Y.: Pergamon Press, 1982.

Curtis, Patricia. *Animal Partners: Training Animals to Help People.* New York: Lodestar/Dutton, 1982.

————. *Cindy: A Hearing-Ear Dog.* New York: E.P. Dutton, 1981.

————. *Greff: The Story of a Guide Dog.* New York: Lodestar/Dutton, 1982.

————. *The Indoor Cat: How to Understand, Enjoy and Care for House Cats.* New York: Doubleday, 1981.

Fitzgerald, Thomas A. *Pet Facilitated Therapy: A Selected Annotated Bibliography.* Denver: The American Humane Association, 1981.

Fogel, Bruce. *Interrelations Between People and Pets.* Springfield, Ill.: Charles Thomas, 1982.

Fox, Michael W. *Between Animal and Man.* New York: Coward, McCann & Geoghegan, 1976.

————. *The Dog: Its Domestication and Behavior.* New York: Garland STMP Press, 1978.

————. *Understanding Your Dog.* New York: Bantam Books, 1977.

Jones, Barbara A. *The Psychology of the Human/Animal Bond: An Annotated Bibliography.* Philadelphia: University of Pennsylvania, 1981.

Lee, Ronnal L., et al. *Guidelines: Animals in Nursing Homes*. Moraga, Calif.: California Veterinary Medical Association, 1983.

Levinson, Boris M. *Pet-Oriented Child Psychotherapy*. Springfield, Ill.: Charles Thomas, 1969.

————. *Pets and Human Development*. Springfield, Ill.: Charles Thomas, 1972.

Lorenz, Konrad Z. *King Solomon's Ring*. New York: Thomas Y. Crowell, 1952.

————. *Man Meets Dog*. Harmondsworth, England: Hazel Watson & Viney, Ltd., 1953.

Lynch, James J. *The Broken Heart*. New York: Basic Books, 1977.

McCowan, Lida L. *It Is Ability That Counts: A Training Manual on Therapeutic Riding for the Handicapped*. Olivet, Mich.: Olivet Press, 1972.

Mery, Fernand. *The Life, History, and Magic of the Cat*. New York: Madison Sq. Press/Grosset & Dunlap, 1972.

Mooney, Samantha. *A Snowflake in My Hand*. New York: Delacorte, 1983.

Sullivan, Tom, with Derek Gill. *If You Could See What I Hear*. New York: Signet, 1976.

————. *You Are Special*. Milwaukee, Wis.: Ideals Publishing Corp., 1980.

Walters, Michelle S. *Maryland Pet Profiles*. Ruxton, Md.: Maryland Publishing Co., 1982.

Whiteside, Robert L. *Animal Language: How to Understand Your Pet*. New York: Frederick Fell, 1981.

Woodhouse, Barbara. *No Bad Dogs: The Woodhouse Way*. New York: Summit Books, 1982.

Yates, E.: *Skeezer: Dog with a Mission*. Irvington-on-Hudson, N.Y.: Harvey House, 1973.

• Bibliography •

Aeschliman, Roger. "Rx for Man: Hug a Pet Twice a Day." *Wichita Eagle*, April 29, 1980.

"Animal Traveling Companions Along the Road to Balanced Mental Health." *American Humane Magazine*, January 1977, pp. 5–7.

Arehart-Treichel, Joan. "Pets: the Health Benefits." *Science News*, March 27, 1982, pp. 220–223.

Arkow, Phil. *How to Start a Pet Therapy Program*. Colorado Springs: Humane Society of the Pikes Peak Region, 1982.

———. *"Pet Therapy": A Study of the Use of Companion Animals in Selected Therapies*. 3rd ed. Colorado Springs: Humane Society of the Pikes Peak Region, 1982.

"Assistance Dog Aiding Handicapped Teen-ager." *ADI Briefly* (Newsletter of Assistance Dogs, Inc.), Spring 1980.

Barrett, Mary Helen. "Mills College Psychology Professor Explores Aspect of Human/Companion Animal Bond." *Latham Letter*, Winter 1981–82. Reprinted from *Mills College Quarterly*.

Beal, Louisa, and Linda Hines. *Annotated Bibliography of the People-Pet Partnership Resource Library*. Alameda, Calif.: Latham Foundation.

Bellamy, William B. "When You Utilize Young Volunteers." *Shoptalk*, March 1974, pp. 4–6.

Berman, Laura. "A Mere Pet May Be Keeping You Healthy." *Detroit Free Press*, October 24, 1980.

"Bill Cosby Helping PAW." *Newburgh* (N.Y.) *Evening News*, November 22, 1981.

"Biomedicine: Bow Wow for Recovery." *Science News*, Vol. 114, No. 24, p. 408.

Blume, Beverly. "The Tie That Binds." *Norden News*, Winter–Spring 1982, pp. 20–28.

Boone, J. Allen. *Kinship with All Life*. New York: Harper & Row, 1954.

Boyd, Cynthia. "Pets May Fill Larger Void Than You Realize." *St. Paul Pioneer Press*, September 16, 1977.

Bridger, Harold. "The Changing Role of Pets in Society." *Journal of Small Animal Practitioner*, 1976, pp. 1–8.

Brody, Jane. "Pets Are Being Used in Varied Therapies." *New York Times*, August 11, 1982.

Bustad, Leo K. *Animals, Aging and the Aged*. Minneapolis: University of Minnesota Press, 1980.

————. "Bethel—An Institution Without Walls." *Latham Letter*, Winter 1981–82, pp. 4–5.

————. "How Animals Make People Human and Humane." *Modern Veterinary Practice*, September 1979, pp. 707–709.

————. "The Peripatetic Dean: People-Pet Partnership." *Western Veterinarian*, Vol. 17, No. 3, 1979, pp. 2–4.

————. "The Peripatetic Dean: Profiling Animals for Therapy." *Western Veterinarian*, Vol. 17, No. 1, 1979, p. 2.

————. "Pets for People Therapy." *Today's Animal Health*, September–October 1978, pp. 8–10.

————, and Linda Hines. "Animal Contributions to the Health and Well-Being of People, Especially the Aged." Presented at JACOPIS conference, September 3, 1980.

————. "Placement of Animals With the Elderly: Benefits and Strategies." *California Veterinarian*, August 1982, pp. 37–44.

Cain, Ann. "A Study of Pets in the Family System." Presented at Georgetown Family Symposium, Washington, D.C., October 27, 1978.

Callister, Scotta. "Get Well by Cuddling Puppy, Says Vet. School Psychiatrist." Corvallis, Ore., *Gazette Times*, December 4, 1980.

"Canine Therapist Sparks Interest at Nursing Home." *Animal-Shelter Shoptalk*, November 1975, pp. 24–25.

Caras, Roger. *A Celebration of Dogs*. New York: Times Books, 1982.

———. "Human Nature: Comforting Creatures." *Science Digest*, June 1981, pp. 14, 118.

Case, Deena B. "People-Pet Relationships." *California Veterinarian*, October 1979, pp. 39–40.

Case, Frederick. "Pets, Prisoners: Partners for Good." *Seattle Times*, July 19, 1982.

"CATS: Putting Kids, Pets and Seniors Together Gets Good Results." *Chelsea* (N.Y.) *Clinton News*, September 4, 1980.

"Center to Study Human-Animal Relationships and Environments Established at University of Minnesota." *Latham Letter*, Winter 1981–82, pp. 3, 11.

Chandler, Edna Walker. "A Special Kind of Graduation." *Dog Fancy*, March 1983, pp. 26–27.

Chase, Ann. "Animal Allies: How They're Helping." *Diabetes Forecast*, July–August 1980, pp. 16–19.

Christy, Duane W. "The Impact of Pets on Children in Placement." *National Humane Review*, April 1974, pp. 6–7.

Condout, A. "For a Biology of Childhood Behavior: The Child's Relationship with Household Pets and Domestic Animals." *Bulletin of French Veterinary Academy*, 1977, Issue 50, pp. 481–490.

Corson, Samuel, and Elizabeth Corson. "Pet-Assisted Psychotherapy." *Mims Magazine*, December 1, 1979, pp. 33–37.

Corson, Samuel A., et al. "Pet Dogs as Non-Verbal Communication Links in Hospital Psychiatry." *Comprehensive Psychiatry*, January–February 1977, pp. 61–72.

————. "The Socializing Role of Pet Animals in Nursing Homes: An Experiment in Nonverbal Communication Therapy." Unpublished paper. June 1976.

Curtis, Patricia. "Animals Are Good for the Handicapped, Perhaps All of Us." *Smithsonian*, July 1981, pp. 49–56.

————. "Our Pets, Ourselves." *Psychology Today*, August 1982.

"A Dog in Residence." A companion-animal study commissioned by JACOPIS, Melbourne, Australia.

"Dogs Like Penny Are Priceless." *Our Animals* (magazine of San Francisco SPCA), Summer–Fall 1982, p. 19.

Doyle, Marina Chapman. "Rabbit—Therapeutic Prescription." *Perspectives in Psychiatric Care*, April–June 1975, pp. 79–82.

Evans, Olive. "Relationships: Even More Than Your Best Friend." *New York Times*, August 17, 1981.

Fales, Edward D., Jr. "Can Pets Help People Get Well— And Stay Well?" *Today's Health*, March 1960, pp. 56–57, 63–64.

Farmer, Frances. *Will There Really Be a Morning?* New York: Putnam's, 1972.

Feldman, Bruce Max. "Why People Own Pets." *Today's Animal Health*, September–October 1979, pp. 22–23.

Fillmore, Gail D. "My Cat, My Therapist." *Cats Magazine*, November 1982, pp. 8, 30.

Fitzgerald, Thomas A. *Pet Facilitated Therapy: A Selected Bibliography*. Denver: American Humane Association, 1981.

Fixx, James J. *The Complete Book of Running*. New York: Random House, 1977.

Flaherty, Joseph A. "Jail Bird." *National Humane Review*, July–August 1958.

Fox, Michael W. "Neuroses in Dogs." *Saturday Review Science*, October 28, 1972, pp. 58–63.

Francis, Gloria. "Animals and Nursing: A Neglected Affair." Unpublished paper.

———. "The Therapeutic Use of Pets." *Nursing Outlook*, June 1981, pp. 369–70.

Freedman, Ray. "Rx for the Mentally Ill." *Dog Fancy*, February 1976, p. 28.

Freiberger, Rema. "Pet Facilitated Psychotherapy." Unpublished paper; summary of talk and subsequent discussion, undated.

———, and Boris Levinson. "Humans and Their Companion Animals in The Family Circle." Unpublished paper.

Friedmann, Erika, et al. "Animal Companions and One-Year Survival of Patients After Discharge from a Coronary Care Unit." *Public Health Reports*, July–August 1980, pp. 304–312.

Froiland, Paul. "Understanding Dolphins." *Passages*, December 1982, pp. 45–50.

Gaunt, John. "A Snowball's Chance." *National Humane Review*, December 1975, pp. 6–7.

Gibbs, Margaret. *Leader Dogs for the Blind*. Fairfax, Va.: Denlinger's, 1982.

"The Gift of the Rainbow." *Our Animals* (magazine of San Francisco SPCA), Summer–Fall 1982, pp. 18, 20.

Gorman, Tom. "Pet Project Aimed at Retarded Children." *Los Angeles Times*, November 28, 1982.

Grenier, P. L. "Prison Cats." *Cat Fancy*, March–April 1972.

Hahn, Emily. "The Peaceable Kingdom." *The New Yorker*, December 28, 1981, pp. 62–67.

Hamilton, Mildred. "Pet Theories About Pet Health." *San Francisco Examiner*, December 15, 1981.

Hamlin, Ann. "Experiences With Companion Animals on a Hospital Ward." Paper presented at Society for Companion Animal Studies' meeting on "Pets and Children," March 19, 1983, London.

"Handi-Dogs for Therapy." *Community Animal Control*, September–October, 1982, pp. 6–8.

Harris, Judy. "Dogs Contribute to Ego Strength: Highlights from an MA Thesis." *Latham Letter*, Winter 1981–82, pp. 2, 13–15.

Harris, Norene. "Betty White's Mailbag." *Animal Cavalcade*, November–December 1972, pp. 18–21.

Harvey, Alice C. "Pets Help Schizophrenics Respond to Outside World." *Clinical Psychiatry News*, May 1982.

Helyar, John. "Talking to Your Dog Can Help to Lower Your Blood Pressure." *Wall Street Journal*, October 16, 1981.

Hines, Linda. "Establishing a People-Pet Partnership Program." Alameda, Calif.: The Latham Foundation.

Holden, Constance. "Human-Animal Relationship Under Scrutiny." *Science*, October 23, 1981, pp. 418–420.

"Hospital, University Establish New Programs Based on Pet Therapy." *Shoptalk*, January 1976, pp. 26–27.

Jernigan, Jean. "Pet Therapy Brings Happiness to the Lonely." *National Humane Review*, November 1973, p. 13.

Jones, Barbara A. "The Psychology of the Human/Companion Animal Bond: An Annotated Bibliography." Philadelphia: University of Pennsylvania, 1981.

Katcher, Aaron Honori. "Interactions Between People and Their Pets: Form and Function." Unpublished paper.

————, and Erika Friedmann. "Potential Health Value of Pet Ownership." *Continuing Education*, February 1980, pp. 117–121.

Katz, Sharon, et al. "Pet Facilitated Therapy: Potential Benefits." *Community Animal Control*, September–October, 1982, pp. 10–11, 20–22.

Kearny, Mathilde. "Pet Therapy." *Massachusetts SPCA Animals*, May–June 1977, pp. 27–29.

Kidd, Aline. "Dogs, Cats and People." *Mills Quarterly*, August 1981, pp. 6–9.

————. "Human Benefits from the Human/Companion Animal Bond." Speech for the Latham Foundation, July 25, 1982.

Kirchmeier, Mark. "Dogs Take New Role as 'Hearing Aids.'" *Sunday Oregonian*, January 8, 1978.

Kirk, Douglas. "Take a Stand Report: Is Pet Ownership Beneficial?" *Dog Fancy*, March 1983, pp. 43–45.

Lapp, Cheryl Ann, and Lynn Scruby. "Responsible Pet Relationships: A Mental Health Perspective." *Health Values*, July–August 1982, pp. 20–25.

LaRiviere, Ann. "Every Rider in This Arena Wins." *Los Angeles Times*, March 21, 1980.

Larsen, Dave. "Hearing Dogs: A Sound Investment." *Los Angeles Times*, May 28, 1982.

————. "Hospital Finds Dog Patients' Best Friend." *Los Angeles Times*, November 23, 1982.

————. "Monkey Trained to Assist Quadriplegic." *Los Angeles Times*, August 17, 1982.

————. "Single Animal Lovers: Birds of a Feather." *Los Angeles Times*, August 9, 1982.

Larson, Charles C. "Your Cat, Your Therapist." *Cats Magazine*, July 1981, p. 14.

LaTour, Kathy. "Serious Monkeyshines." *American Way*, November 1980, pp. 142–144.

Lauda, Frani. "Pet Therapy Eases Tensions in Lorton Reformatory." Press release; New York: Niki Singer, Inc.

Leigh, Denis. "The Psychology of the Pet Owner." *Small Animal Practitioner*, Vol. 7, 1966, pp. 517–521.

Lescher, Steven. "Horses Help the Handicapped." *Western Horseman*, November 1973, pp. 18, 117–118.

Levinson, Boris M. "Children Need Pets." *Pet Fair*, August 1969, pp. 21, 46.

————. "The Dog as a 'Co-therapist.'" *Mental Hygiene*, January 1962, pp. 59–65.

————. "Nursing Home Pets: A Psychological Adventure for the Patient." *National Humane Review*, July–August 1970, pp. 14–16.

————. "The Pet and the Child's Bereavement." *Mental Hygiene*, April 1967, pp. 197–200.

————. *Pet Oriented Child Psychotherapy.* Springfield, Ill.: Charles Thomas, 1969.

————. "Pets and Modern Family Life." *National Humane Review*, January 1973, pp. 5–9.

————. "Pets—A New Way to Help Disturbed Children." *Parents Magazine*, September 22, 1968.

————. "Some Observations on the Use of Pets in Psycho-diagnosis." *Pediatrics Digest*, April 1966, pp. 81–85.

————. "Therapeutic Value of Pet Ownership Is Vast." *Pets/Supplies/Marketing*, June 1971, pp. 61–64.

Linder, Lee. "People Feel Better If Talking to a Bird, Watching Fish Swim." *Baltimore Evening Sun*, October 30, 1980.

MacDonald, Alisdair J. "Attachment Theory." *Group for the Study of the Human/Companion Animal Bond Newsletter*, Vol. 2, No. 1 (1981), pp. 14–16.

————. "Review: Children and Companion Animals." *Child Care, Health and Development*, 1979, pp. 347–358.

————. "The Role of Pets in the Mental Health of Children." Unpublished paper for Group for the Study of the Human/Companion Animal Bond, Dundee, Scotland, 1979.

MacKneson, Ruth. "Pets—Helping People Cope." *Toronto Humane Society Humane Viewpoint*, Summer 1980, pp. 6–7.

"Man's Best Medicine." Segment of *60 Minutes*; transcript of broadcast of October 3, 1982; CBS News.

Manual, Diane Casselberry. "Animals Win Hearts, Influence People, Says Pet Expert." *Christian Science Monitor*, December 15, 1981, p. 18.

McCowan, Lida L. *It Is Ability That Counts: A Training Manual on Therapeutic Riding for the Handicapped.* Olivet, Mich.: Olivet Press, 1972.

McCulloch, Michael J. "Animal Facilitated Therapy: Overview and Future Direction." *California Veterinarian*, August 1982, pp. 13–24.

————. "The Pet as Prothesis—Defining Criteria for Adjunctive Use of Companion Animals in the Treatment of Medically Ill, Depressed Outpatients." Paper, 1981.

McCulloch, William F., and Michael J. McCulloch. "The Practicing Veterinarian—Contributions to Comparative Medicine." *Southwestern Veterinarian*, Vol. 29, No. 3 (1976), pp. 212–216.

Messent, Peter R. "Behavior Patterns of Companion Animals: Their Significance in Pet/Owner Bonding." Paper for Meeting on Pet/Owner Bond, Dundee, Scotland, March 25, 1979.

————. "Increase in People-Pet Contacts Through Dogs as Social Catalysts." Speech presented at 20th International Congress of Applied Psychology, Edinburgh, Scotland, July 25–31, 1982.

————. "A Review of Recent Developments in Human-

Companion Animal Studies." *Proceedings of the Kal-Kan Symposium*, September 26–27, 1981.

Morrison, Patt. "Muggins Arrives—It's the Best Medicine for Cancer Patient, 12." *Los Angeles Times*, October 25, 1982.

Mugford, Roger A. "The Contributions of Pets to Human Development." Paper, February 1977.

"National Humane Review Attends a Pet Show for Handicapped Youngsters." *National Humane Review*, March–April, 1966, pp. 10–11.

North American Riding for the Handicapped Association, Inc. *Annual Report and Journal, 1982–83.*

"Notes on the Inaugural Seminar of the Joint Advisory Committee on Pets in Society." Meeting held in Melbourne, Australia, September 3, 1980.

"Old Folks Need Their Pets." *National Humane Review*, September–October 1969, p. 3.

Packard, Vance. *A Nation of Strangers*. New York: David McKay, 1972.

Peerson, Janet. "Next Miracle Drug May Be the Family Pet." *The News World*, October 28, 1981.

Perrow, Julanne Allison. "Hearing Dogs." *Dog Fancy*, March 1983, pp. 34–35.

"Pet Day at the Falls Nursing Home." *Animal Shelter Shoptalk*, May 1976, pp. 4–5.

"Pet Facilitated Therapy." *National Animal Protection Newsletter*, Winter 1982, p. 4.

"Pet Placement Program Involves Senior Citizens." *Animal Shelter Shoptalk*, December 1974.

"Pet Prescriptions: An Emerging Therapy." *Journal of the American Veterinary Medical Association*, November 15, 1980.

"Pets As a Social Phenomenon: A Study of Man-Pet Interaction in Urban Communities." Report by Petcare Information and Advisory Service, Melbourne, Australia.

"Pets Behind Bars." *Spokane Chronicle*, July 19, 1982.

"Pets by Prescription: A Novel Program of Minnesota Humane Society." *Colorado State Department of Public Health, Public Veterinary Section*, November 1, 1972, p. 971.

"Pets Can Ease the After-Shocks of Retirement." Press release, Pets Are Wonderful Council, Chicago.

"Pets, People and Public Housing." *Our Animals*, Winter 1981, pp. 3, 6, 9.

Quinn, Kathy. "Dogs for Therapy." *Pure-Bred Dogs American Kennel Gazette*, September 1979, pp. 38–41.

Roberts, Chris. "Pets Aid Psychological Treatment." *Rocky Mountain News*, "Now" (Denver, Colo.), December 16, 1979.

Robin, Michael. "A Study of the Relationship of Childhood Pet Animals and the Psycho-Social Development of

Adolescents." Summary of University of Minnesota study. Pets Are Wonderful Council, Chicago.

Rosenblatt, Rae Marie. "When Society's Strays—Men and Cats—Meet in Prison." *National Humane Review*, August 1976, pp. 14–15.

Ross, Geraldine. "Chum . . . Turtle with a Mission." *National Humane Review*, July 1974, pp. 12–13.

Ross, Samuel B., Jr. "Children and Companion Animals." *Ross Timesaver* (newsletter, Ross Laboratories, Columbus, Ohio), July–August 1981, pp. 13, 16.

————. "The Therapeutic Use of Animals with the Handicapped." Paper, Green Chimneys Children's Services, Brewster, N.Y., Spring 1983.

Roswell, Harry, and A. A. McWilliam. "Anguish and Grief: Helping the Aged to Cope with the Loss of a Pet." Ottawa: Canadian Council on Animal Care.

Rovner, Judy. "Self-Help: Happiness Is a Warm Kitten." *Washington Post*, November 26, 1981.

"Senior Pets for Senior Citizens." *Brief Paws*, Summer 1980.

Serpell, James A. "Growing Up with Pets and Its Influence on Adult Attitude." Unpublished paper.

"Sounding the Alert." *Our Animals*, Winter 1981, pp. 6–7, 14–15.

"Special Training Builds Youngsters' Self-Confidence." *Shoptalk*, August 1973.

Storch, Dorothy. "Ever Ponder Why People Who Like Pets Are More Personable?" *Houston Post*, October 17, 1981.

Stratthaus, Theresa. "Meant for Each Other." *Guideposts*, December 1982, pp. 20–23.

Tapscott, Joey. "Lady of the Cages." *National Humane Review*, January–February 1970, pp. 4–6.

Taylor, Lesley. "Humans Benefit from Having Pets, Group Finds." *Bucyrus* (Ohio) *Telegraph-Forum*, November 7, 1981.

"Training Club Assumes Pet Therapy Program." *Animal Shelter Shoptalk*, July 1975.

Trussel, Vicky L. "Lima State Hospital: People Helping Animals Helping People." *American Humane Magazine*, June 1978.

———. "More on Pet Therapy for the Mentally Ill." *Today's Animal Health*, July–August 1979, pp. 22–23.

"Try a Little T.L.C." *Science '80*, January–February 1980.

"Use of Animals in Psychotherapy with Children." Paper presented at the Annual Meeting of the Federated Humane Societies of Pennsylvania, Allentown, September 20, 1968.

Voell, Paula. "You Can Teach an Old Dog New Tricks." *Buffalo* (N.Y.) *Evening News*, September 23, 1981.

Von Kreisler-Bomben, Kristen. "The Hearing Ear Dog." *Today's Animal Health*, March–April 1980, pp. 14–15.

Walster, Dorothy. "Pets and the Elderly." Unpublished paper, dated March 18, 1973.

————. "Pets and the Elderly." *Latham Letter*, Summer 1982, pp. 1, 3, 17.

————. "The Role of Pets in the Mental Health of the Elderly." Scottish Health Education Unit, March 1979.

————. "The Two-Way Benefits That Companion Animals Bring to Children and the Elderly." *Group for the Study of the Human/Companion Animal Bond Newsletter*, Vol. 1, No. 3 (1981), pp. 2–5.

Walters, Michelle S. *Maryland Pet Profiles*. Ruxton, Md.: Maryland Publishing Company, 1982.

Warren, Ken. "The Queen of State Prison." *American Humane Magazine*, August 1977, p. 15.

"Warning: Living Alone Is Dangerous to Your Health—Interview with James J. Lynch." *U.S. News & World Report*, June 20, 1977.

Weaver, Peter. "Pet Therapy—Bringing Shut-Ins out of Their Shells." *Washington Post*, February 5, 1978.

Whitaker, Helen. "Dogs for Therapy." *Dog Fancy*, December 1979, pp. 26–27.

White, Ken. "Animals: Partners in Helping and Healing." *San Francisco SPCA/Quarterly Journal*, Winter 1980, pp. 5, 8.

Wolff, Ethel. "A Survey of the Use of Animals in Psychotherapy in the United States." Paper prepared for the American Humane Association, September 30, 1977.

Yoxall, A. T., and Dorothy M. Yoxall. "Pet Animal-Owner Interactions: The Multidisciplinary Approach." Paper, for Group for the Study of the Human-Companion Animal Bond, Dundee, Scotland, 1979.

· Index ·